# More Praise for *The Power of*

"John Schuster's latest book ev[...] cated and colorful pasts and o[...] reveled in, appreciated, and lea[...] focusing on the future or living so[...] [...] access our pasts as a rich lode of insight and guidance! Schuster is a master coach and master storyteller; this book should be read by everyone concerned with human change."
—**Doug Silsbee, author of *Presence-Based Coaching***

"A great new way of thinking that will enable our leaders to use their past creatively in order to better live their present and robustly lean into their future."
—**Carmen M. Allison, Head of Executive Development, Gap Inc.**

"Schuster doesn't stop with observations about how our pasts can be effective tools for creating our desired future. He gives us practical steps to reveal the watershed events of our pasts and then gain new insights into who we are, who and what we can be, and how we can chart our own paths forward."
—**Doug Robinette, CEO, Integros Coaching and Consulting, and former President, Nationwide Insurance Operations**

"John helps us to reflect on how we are stuck in the present, focusing on a ruthless and unpredictable future, neglecting our history and our past. It's amazing how he touches us with the most intriguing question of our lives: Where did I come from, who I am, and where do I go?"
—**José Augusto Figueiredo, COO, DBM Latin America, and President, International Coach Federation Brazil**

"This book helps look at the sources of the power and imagination that all true leaders possess. Leaders need to know the beginning of their journey to leadership if they hope to help others on theirs."
—**Earl Walker, former Dean, School of Business Administration, The Citadel**

"John Schuster brings to light a valuable, introspective insight that will cause you to breathe more deeply and act with greater confidence and clarity. John's message around acknowledging and embracing the value of our past is powerful."
—**Dave Goebel, CEO, Mr. Goodcents; Merryck Mentor; and former CEO, Applebee's**

"Schuster's book brilliantly emphasizes the power of coming home to our own very personal history and harvesting what's essential while recasting the adversities. He challenges the 'be here now' mentality and provides a clear road map for adjusting the course and using our history to strengthen life in the present!"

—**Pamela McLean, PhD, CEO, The Hudson Institute of Santa Barbara**

"A clear and precise guide for working with clients to unearth the things that matter from their history, both the gifts needing to be recalled (performance-enhancing thinking and resources) and lessons from negative experiences recast to enable forward movement (performance-interfering thinking), yet Schuster makes clear these methods are *not* a replacement for therapy."

—**Terrence E. Maltbia, EdD, Senior Lecturer, Teachers College, Columbia University, and Faculty Director, The Columbia Coaching Certification Program**

"John has enabled many leaders to achieve beyond their expectations. This book will lead them to go beyond themselves again. I so recommend this book for all those who want to align themselves with their best contributions and work, including the meaning of their financial success."

—**Bob Rogers, former Chairman and CEO, Ewing Marion Kauffman Foundation**

"Without proper reflection we are prone to repeat mistakes and unable to reach our full potential. In this book, John Schuster gives readers the means to tap into their past and create their future, thereby increasing their odds of success. Spend the time to understand the power of your past—you will be richer for it."

—**Stan Sword, Vice President of Total Rewards, Sprint Nextel Corporation**

"In a work of uncommon grace and insight, Schuster reminds us of our personal and collective tendencies toward misunderstanding, misinterpreting, and misremembering. He explains what it is that takes place, why this matters, and how we can make use of this knowledge in order to grow as successful human beings."

—**Larry C. Spears, President, The Spears Center for Servant-Leadership**

"A skillful interweaving of depth psychology, leadership development, and care for the soul."

—**Scott Harrison, Director of Developer and Software Partner Programs, Intel Corporation, and executive coach**

# The Power of Your Past

Other books by John P. Schuster

*Answering Your Call: A Guide to Living Your Deepest Purpose*

*The Power of Open-Book Management*

*The Open-Book Management Field Book*

*From Hum-Drum to Hot-Diggity on Leadership*

# The Power of Your Past

## The Art of Recalling, Reclaiming, and Recasting

### John P. Schuster

Berrett–Koehler Publishers, Inc.
San Francisco
*a BK Life book*

Berrett-Koehler Publishers, Inc.
235 Montgomery Street, Suite 650
San Francisco, CA 94104-2916
Tel: (415) 288-0260      Fax: (415) 362-2512      www.bkconnection.com

ORDERING INFORMATION
*Quantity sales.* Special discounts are available on quantity purchases by cor-
porations, associations, and others. For details, contact the "Special Sales
Department" at the Berrett-Koehler address above.
*Individual sales.* Berrett-Koehler publications are available through most
bookstores. They can also be ordered directly from Berrett-Koehler: Tel: (800)
929-2929; Fax: (802) 864-7626; www.bkconnection.com
*Orders for college textbook/course adoption use.* Please contact Berrett-
Koehler: Tel: (800) 929-2929; Fax: (802) 864-7626.
*Orders by U.S. trade bookstores and wholesalers.* Please contact Ingram Publisher Services, Tel: (800) 509-4887; Fax: (800) 838-1149; E-mail: customer
.service@ingrampublisherservices.com; or visit www.ingrampublisherservices
.com/Ordering for details about electronic ordering.

Berrett-Koehler and the BK logo are registered trademarks of Berrett-Koehler
Publishers, Inc.

PRINTED IN THE UNITED STATES OF AMERICA
Berrett-Koehler books are printed on long-lasting acid-free paper. When it is
available, we choose paper that has been manufactured by environmentally
responsible processes. These may include using trees grown in sustainable
forests, incorporating recycled paper, minimizing chlorine in bleaching, or
recycling the energy produced at the paper mill.

LIBRARY OF CONGRESS CATALOGING-IN-PUBLICATION DATA
Schuster, John P.
  The power of your past : the art of recalling, reclaiming and recasting / by
John P. Schuster. — 1st ed.
    p. cm.
  Includes index.
  ISBN 978-1-60509-826-5 (pbk.)
  1. Career development—Psychological aspects. 2. Recollection (Psychology)
3. Reminiscing. 4. Self-perception. 5. Self-realization. I. Title.
  HF5381.S4235 2011
  650.1--dc22                      2010050189

FIRST EDITION
16  15  14  13  12  11          10  9  8  7  6  5  4  3  2  1

INTERIOR DESIGN & ILLUSTRATION: Gopa&Ted2 Design
COPYEDITOR: Elissa Rabellino          INDEXER: Mary Heinrich
COVER DESIGN: pemastudio          PROOFREADER: Henrietta Bensussen
BOOK PRODUCER: Linda Jupiter Productions

To Rita Schuster and Audrey Kane,
moms with memories of gold and silver,
and to aunt Dorothy Cunningham,
keeper of the treasure of laughs.

# Contents

# Preface

I GOT USED TO her laugh by being around it all the time. My friends would remind me how special it was—"Wow, that is one great laugh your mom has." What it carried was joy to the max. It both created, and was carried by, a big happy bandwidth. Rita was a small person, but she had a set of overcapacity, drill-sergeant lungs.

When she was on her deathbed at age 92, I heard what was left of her laugh in her diminished state. She had kept the laugh, and its roots—the stance toward life of finding the fun everywhere—until the end of her days. I had my last hour with Mom on her last full day of partial consciousness. She'd fade in and out some, but she knew me and my two sisters, and we spent the day holding her hand and conversing.

In my last hour with her alone, I pulled out my guitar and played and sang. I had heard that music soothes the dying. After one song, she surprised me with a very clear "That was a good performance," the last words she ever spoke to me.

It occurred to me, while holding her hand, to go over the memories that she had cherished all her life and told and retold, often from different angles, one last time. These memories had become one of her life sources of joy and meaning. I said things like, "Remember that huge windstorm up in

Wisconsin at Bud's house? We cut through four trees the next day just to get our car out of the driveway." I recalled a memory of her recalling memories. "Remember you and Dorothy and Helen (her sisters) sitting on the porch in Iowa under the stars, telling stories about the Cunninghams' life on the farm? Remember the time Dorothy jumped onto the fat bull snake, *barefoot*? ... Remember ... ?" She kept smiling and nodding, eyes still sparkling.

I did in that last hour what I had learned from her. I harvested her past in a final sweep of rich memories. We relished the stories of her life with her husband, Paul, and her siblings. Very soon after we had reviewed the constellation of images that made up her interior world and brought her laugh to life, she went out of consciousness.

## Why This Book

Rita would like it that she helped to inspire a book about making our yesterdays a resource that we can call upon now and in our uncertain, full-of-possibilities future. In addition to having been her son, I am a father and grandpa, an author, a teacher of executive coaching, and a mentor to leaders. I live in the Midwest and the East, was born in rural Iowa like Rita, and worked in leadership development with corporations, nonprofits, and government for over 30 years.

This book was born out of that work and study. I noticed early on how well most effective people had defined themselves using their personal history. And I also noticed the opposite—how less-effective people were usually fuzzy about their yesterdays. It became time to write when I clearly saw that what was so important was not obvious to most.

I did not write this book to talk about the impact of the generations before you. That is an important topic but not in the scope of this book. Nor is it about past lives, if you are into that kind of thinking. It is about your personal history starting at day one, breath one.

Much is being taught on presence in the moment, on the benefits and processes for staying in the now, that is both widespread and very useful. You may have read some of the books on this movement or at least heard about it. I have benefited from this thinking in many ways. It is my contention, however, that presence is only half the story. In this book, I want to fill in the other half. We cannot afford to miss the half on our past.

This book is about using your past creatively in order to better live your present and to robustly lean into your future. It describes how to fix the underuse and misuse of the building blocks of our lives, our yesterdays. It is a systematic and creative guide to making your past sing and play and work for you. And your yesterdays can indeed do all of those things.

This trek into your past is the primary means to both mine your hidden gold and reprogram your hidden self-limiting beliefs. It is not about planning and goal-setting your way to your future, which you already know how to do.

*Planning your way through the limits that stem from your yesterdays is like dynamiting your way through cobwebs—the wrong tool, and likely to do more damage than good.*

Our mind and will set goals and plans within whatever context we provide them. What we work on here is the context of our thinking and willing, and so we put energy into structures more foundational than planning. When we fully harvest our past, we provide a rich context for moving forward. Our career and life plans can best emerge from the core places in our being. With clarity on our personal history, we can access the wellspring of our truest contributions and the source of our best decisions for our larger life journey.

In this work on your yesterdays, then, expect something different. The aim of this book is to rework your memories, and the helpful and less-than-helpful lessons stemming from them, so that you can imagine and practice new ways of being, doing, and loving. Are there other ways to advance your self-knowledge and self-awareness? Of course—many valuable ones. This treatment, however, concerns one very important way that is undervalued and poorly taught.

*This book is about re-possibilitizing. It is about gathering important insights, and the wisdom that comes before informed action.*

## Who Should Read This Book: The Stuck, the Curious, the Successful, the Helping Professions

This book is written for working people, for leaders and professionals and sole proprietors and nonprofit managers, for teachers and those in health care, for artists—for all those who want to open up new possibilities for living, with an emphasis on their work life.

I wrote it for people who already have dynamic careers and for those who may be stuck and not moving. In a comic strip some years back, Dilbert responds to a simple "How is work?" question from his mom by saying, "Incompetence hangs in the air like the cold stench of death. I'm drowning, and monkeys dressed as lifeguards are throwing me anvils."

If you have caught any anvils recently, this book is for you.

And it is also very much meant for the anvil-free who experience work success, and who have put useful professional and personal growth practices in place.

A premise of this book is that no matter where you are on the spectrum of life's success-o-meter, even at the top, there is still work with your past, good work, that will add value to your current and future life.

So if you are at the top with

> *a million or two in savings, a perfect partner, great health and good looks, fun kids, and a career filled with ever more promise,*

or in the middle with

> *a good middle-class life with a little savings, a healthy lifestyle, pretty good looks, a career that is more steady than spectacular, a stable partner, and a mortgage that won't bury you,*

or nearer the bottom with

> *too much debt, aches and stiffness, marginal looks, an unreliable car, a dead-end job with two outplacements behind you, kids who ignore you, and a relationship in serious need of some romance and zest,*

no matter where you are on that spectrum, this book adds value and important perspective. The outside of your life, as measured by the success-o-meter, is a weak indicator at best of what still lies in your stored-up bank account of yesterdays that you can harvest to enhance and improve your life today and tomorrow. This book does not ignore the outside of your life, but it starts and ends with the inside, with your thoughts and your beliefs and all the mental-emotional-spiritual dynamics that determine the outside, as measured by the success-o-meter. This is about your inner theater and about you as the playwright.

Many of you have already taken action to grow. You attend professional or personal workshops, or you access faith-based or other forms of spiritual resources, or you engage a coach. These activities are so useful and will be markedly accelerated if your lessons from your yesterdays pop with the power of their singular truths.

**When people encounter the deep currents of their unique path, that is where substantial growth resides.**

It is rare that even the highly successful, who are usually overbusy with success, have fully and creatively mined their unique history or know what their particular amalgamation of memories can mean and do for them.

## A Special Word for the Helpers—
## Coaches and Counselors

Some people may be in a hindering profession, though I have yet to meet one. Many of us claim to be in the human development and helping professions. This book is meant for the general working professional and not exclusively for development/helping professionals. Still, if you are a counselor, therapist, or leadership developer, you will find ideas that you can use for your clients.

This is not written as a coaching book, but if you are a coach, you will still find ways to use it. As you know, we coaches focus more on the present and future than most therapists, but we assist our clients regularly by fighting off the faulty thinking and views that leak from their past into their present, inhibiting their achievement of worthwhile efforts. So don't think of it as a coaching book, but use it as you will and tell me what happens.

## THE MANY PEOPLE WHO TALKED TO ME ABOUT THEIR PAST

In addition to years of observation and working with hundreds on the concepts presented in this book, I directly interviewed 14 individuals (and surveyed approximately 30 more). The list includes guitarist and performer Tommy Emmanuel; John Pepper, former CEO of Procter & Gamble; Gifford Pinchot, social entrepreneur and thought leader for innovation and sustainable business; Valerie Morris, CNN anchor for 15 years; and David Dotlich, author and leadership development guru. You will hear many of their stories. This is not meant to be a research book, but the positions I take and thoughts I emphasize come from more than my experience—they come from others' as well.

## HOW TO READ THIS BOOK: SELF-REFLECTION ON THE WHOLE OF YOU

Don't be in any kind of hurry to read this book. This is more a slow-read book than a fast-read book, even though it is chunked into small, digestible parts for easy access. Speed is not the enemy here, but it can hamper many kinds of growth. Set the book down after you hit a part that resonates; look out the window at 35,000 feet, across the crowded parking lot at your condo, or above the heads of the folks who slipped onto the subway with you; and think about what you just read.

To reap the most from this book will take self-reflection with heart. You will gain much as you muster up the will to take a look at your life, your work, and your past and its meanings. The examples and methods will support your quest for self-knowledge that matters.

Splitting people into an artificial dichotomy of the person at work and the person in her personal life can cause problems. For the purpose of this book, then, we will touch on your personal life and harvest memories of events that occurred before the work stage of life. I will concentrate the majority of applications in the book, however, on work life.

When we use the term *work*, keep in mind that we are not only talking about your job. This book's focus is on any role that you care about, especially as you want to have a positive impact on the world of work and your community. Your role as a part-time artist or parent may currently hold the bigger promise of a contribution and grab the bigger share of your heart and imagination. I will often use the word *lifework* to designate your work and life and any role within a career or outside of it. We maintain a whole-person perspective throughout. By focusing on work, however, we enjoy the boundaries that come with a primary application.

## The Flow of the Book

The book has three parts. The first, comprising chapters 1 and 2, describes how and why we miss, through a kind of forgetting, the learning from our yesterdays. This cultural blind spot carries a big cost. A bit of theory describes the dynamics of how the assets and limits from our past get deposited in our memories, and how powerful that is for our current lives and work.

The second part, comprising chapters 3, 4, and 5, is the how-to part of the book. It takes you through the steps for reclaiming the assets and recasting the lessons. This section describes the methods you can apply to your current settings.

The third part, comprising chapters 6 and 7, addresses two big issues: (1) How can I strike the balance of fitting in the world while making sure that I am uniquely my own person? (2) How can I acquire wisdom when I face life's biggest challenges? This is answered in the last chapter.

## Amnesia, Core Ideas, Affirmations, and Exercises

Each chapter has core features. The amnesia vignettes at the start briefly explore how movies and books have portrayed the damaging impact of disruption with our past. The core ideas at the end are the distilled lesson of the chapter. The statements of intent at the end are affirmations aimed at creating an inner resonance to move you ahead. Use these statements. Read them aloud. Print them out and tape them to your computer screen, your bathroom mirror. They act as a fuel additive, poured into the tank of your positive restlessness and yearning. They will help you burn cleaner while you go about learning, growing, serving, and having fun.

At the end of the chapters that do not have exercises at their core, I provide questions and/or exercises so that you can apply the concepts and reflect as we go. Address the ones to which you are drawn, and of course make up your own.

## THE FINAL MYSTERY

After my mom and I shared some words on that cold February day, I left the sparse room knowing that we had enjoyed our last living connection. Many thoughts, questions, and feelings swirled around in my head and heart. I still carry one question with me: How can we live more like my mom, all the way to the end, with a joy for living that others feel, always?

We cannot address all of the mysteries that such a question conjures up, but we can address some. I am eager, after years of data gathering and thinking, to go down that path with you.

May we all harvest our powerful past in creative and life-enhancing ways.

John P. Schuster
Columbus, Ohio
November 2010

*Do not be afraid of the past. If people tell you that it is irrevocable, do not believe them. The past, the present and the future are but one moment in the sight of God.... Time and space ... are merely accidental conditions of a thought. The imagination can transcend them.... Things, also, are in their essence what we choose to make them.*

—OSCAR WILDE, *DE PROFUNDIS*

# Introduction:
# Your Past Can Work for You

*A common story line for movies and novels is the amnesia-stricken hero, who doesn't know who he is or how he got to wherever the story starts. We meet him as he embarks on a quest to find out his story.*

*We are all that character. In the movies, the amnesia is total. Our amnesia is partial. Either way, the effect of the amnesia is a kind of disorientation. We know that we are somewhere, doing something, and we wonder why. In the movies, a sinister secret spy agency or a trauma to the head is the common origin of the amnesia. In our case, the origin is a culture that encourages us to disconnect from our past and focus on the present and future.*

*You are the hero here. You are about to go on a quest to overcome amnesia by harnessing the power of your past and clarifying your identity and direction. Amnesia is a metaphor; your being a hero is not.*

M ANY OF US don't have a useful, full relationship with our past, the kind that could inform us for a lifetime. We avoid the difficult parts and underuse the enriching parts, when we could draw lessons and energy from both. We find ways to demonize, sentimentalize, ignore, forget, and more.

What we don't know does indeed hurt us. We don't know what we don't know about our collective underuse and misuse of our past. We don't know what our personal history can do for us or how our amnesia carries such a big price tag in life and work. The price is paid at different times and in different ways, but it is always paid in full.

I recently witnessed a seven-year-veteran vice president of a large enterprise getting fired for his collective acts of self-delusion, ones that had grown more dramatic over time as he refused to confront his inner scam. He blamed and undermined the boss artfully at first, and then increasingly recklessly. He subtly and then not-so-subtly manipulated his employees' impressions, and hid the contracts that weren't working. It all went up in flames of indignation that he could be so underappreciated when his "incompetent" boss delivered the termination.

Some false story he had started spinning about his capabilities and his role, born of past failures to accept feedback and see the truth, became the fiction that led to his demise. Among other things, he pictured himself as the smartest guy in the room and felt that being reared in a tough environment with ample money gave him an edge over his rural-born, middle-class boss. He wasn't, and it didn't.

This executive's behavior is an example of what Bill George, former CEO of Medtronic, describes as flawed leadership: "Many leaders . . . leave little room for self-exploration. . . . Often, [they can] be successful for a while, but it [leaves] them highly vulnerable, as their lack of self-awareness can lead to major mistakes and errors in judgment."[1] The seven-year veteran was all of these: vulnerable and without enough awareness to see his huge errors in judgment.

**Don't let our speed-addicted, now-biased culture's widespread ignorance about the gifts of the past keep you from harvesting the lessons of yesterday and putting them into the hands of the person who can use them wisely—you. Your yesterdays are a fount of guidance and lessons that can energize you throughout your life, if you know how to tap them.**

When we approach our yesterdays with the courage to confront their truths and the imagination to expand on their lessons, then we move into our future equipped with richly sculpted identities.

This collective amnesia exists for a reason: many argue that the past has no value. None other than Eckhart Tolle, who has a sizable following, starts out his popular book on the importance of staying in the moment, *The Power of Now*, with this sentence: "I have little use for the past and rarely think about it."[2] And then he argues for a few hundred pages on why now is the only source of real human potency.

"Little use for the past"? This is an extreme position to take and feels like a loss—and, in many instances, an outright danger. Our yesterdays are a rich vein for learning and more, if we use them well. We all sense the validity of Santayana's axiom, "Those who cannot remember the past are condemned to repeat it."[3]

I contend that an easier and more fruitful way to improve our awareness is to do what we do naturally, which is to scan our past, creatively. Our memories are more important than doing mental gymnastics on behalf of all-powerful nowness. Our history is richer and more useful as a resource than pretending we don't have it. I grant Mr. Tolle that in one sense, now is all we have, and I would grant him that many of us attend to our history quite poorly. Yes, we can get stuck in our stories as we repeat them.[4] But that in no way means that we should not regularly dip into our yesterdays with awareness and care, learning what we can from them and drawing inspiration and self-definition.

Niels Bohr, the early-20th-century physicist, said that the opposite of one profound truth is another profound truth. It is the dynamic tensions between polar opposites that hold the field of truth. So this book will provide the truth opposing nowness.

**The dynamic truth is that now and yesterday are of equal power and value.**

Using your past well is not a cakewalk, but it is easier for most, and I would say more fruitful, than nowing-it-out at all times, minimizing the lessons of your yesterdays. More on this when we discuss our underused past.

## THE PRICE: WHAT YOU ARE UNAWARE OF CONTROLS YOU

The failure to understand the truth of our yesterdays leads to errors in judgment and a significant sapping of our energy. It robs us of the very power that life yearns to have flow through us. Each denial and misassessment, even the small ones, has a cost. Collectively, they go far beyond any price we think we may be paying. This amnesia-caused mistaken sense of ourselves creates major obstacles in three important areas:

- ► *Identity:* We fall short of identifying who we are and what we are here to do.
- ► *Potential:* It lessens the expression of our unique capacities and our ability to make a difference.
- ► *Self-direction:* It allows us to be influenced by others and the social messages around us rather than charting our own course.

Not knowing how to harness the power of yesterday is an honest-to-goodness showstopper. It is a game ender, a crying-out-loud shame, a mission mangler.

**If the underlying falsehood of the immature person is failure to accept personal responsibility, then task number one in life is to see and claim the truth about ourselves.**

I vividly remember the woman at a workshop who came up to me at a break and said, "I feel like a puddle compared with my husband." My heart got a bit caught in my throat at this offhand self-destructive description. The image of her negatively comparing herself to a puddle will never leave me—what a devastating self-assessment, at what cost, devoid of any realization of her inner beauty, gifts, or opportunities to be uniquely herself in the world. Without any more information, we can all sense how the puddle image damages her identity, her potential, and her self-direction. What in her distant and more recent past had driven her to such a conclusion?

## TRANSFORMING THE MOMENT THROUGH REDISCOVERING YESTERDAY

Misinterpreting your past is one thing. Using it really well is another. Let me give you a few examples.

You can't be around Tommy Emmanuel, whom many think is the world's greatest guitarist, without getting infected by his enthusiasm.[5] He is contagious with possibilities, the beauty of music, and laughter. And he has a million and one stories from his past. When I interviewed him, he shared this one.

66 I came over here in 1980 [from Australia]. I was 25, I came to America the first time. I remember I was sitting in Chet Atkins's office waiting for him to come downstairs . . . and it hit me like a ton of bricks where I was. I'd made it to America and I was sitting in Chet Atkins's office. And for a second I kind of had a small panic attack and thinking, "Oh my God, what if I just sound like a terrible version of him?" You know what I mean? And he'll go, "Oh, no, not another one." And I panicked for a second.

And when he came in the room, he put his arm around me and a sense of peace really came over me immediately, and he said, "Do you want to pick a little?" . . . And I started playing

"Me and Bobby McGee." And he's watching me really closely. And I'm trying to play well for my idol, my hero, my mentor. And he says, "I didn't do that, I didn't do that," and he's pointing to all these things that I'm doing. It was his way of saying, "You're doing your own thing." And it was a really great moment. And I learned. . . . It hit me years later when I was talking about that, I suddenly realized, "Wow! He never said, 'You play just like me.' He said, 'I didn't do that.' And it dawned on me what he'd done. And he sent me away 10 feet tall.[6] 🙶

It was years after that first encounter with the incomparable Chet Atkins that Tommy realized the full power of what Chet had given him. Tommy's memory, not affected by amnesia, contains this story and thousands more, from what I could tell by being with him at guitar camp.[7] His passion for guitar fully links to his memories of his life and of the gifts he received, and to the gift he is to the world of music.

I know a female entrepreneur from South America who worked for the United Nations in her 20s before starting her own business in Manhattan. In a recent distressed state of overwork and being stretched too thin, she needed to remind herself of why she put up with these hassles of entrepreneurship. As her mentor, I evoked a salient memory of the time she single-handedly, totally outside of her job duties, rewired a floor of the United Nations for some new IT capacity, rather than waiting for the bureaucracy to respond. This incident, the 25-year-old version of her taking charge, making up her own rules as she went along, revivified in her imagination the core path for her life's work. She was bound to go the route, rocky at times, of an entrepreneur forging her own way in the volatile financial services industry.

## REMEMBRANCE: THE PROCESS FOR CAPTURING THE POWER OF YESTERDAY

The process we will use for tapping the power of our past is *remembrance*, the willful act of imaginative remembering to overcome any form of amnesia. Remembrance includes three distinct phases: *recalling*, *reclaiming*, and *recasting*:

1. *Recalling*—mapping our unique past
2. *Reclaiming*—amplifying lessons from the positives
3. *Recasting*—reinterpreting lessons from the negatives

Your past should sing and play and work for you, like it does for Tommy Emmanuel. The remembrance process, which is a guided tour of your yesterdays, will most likely also make you sweat some—recalling, reclaiming, and recasting is not a one-way coast downhill. It might even make you bleed a little, in a good way, as you come in deeper contact with your core.

Many authors include exercises that have readers delve into their past. Books on improving your relationships, on money matters, and on food issues often include a section on getting at the origins of your limited current thinking that is causing underperformance and problems. These are piecemeal approaches to our yesterdays because of their singular focus, and they most often are getting at the negatives without fully appreciating the positives. These authors have a feeling for our accepted amnesia and forgetfulness. They sense the power latent in the past with payoffs for our identity, potential, and self-direction, but don't have a full appreciation of remembrance as we will use it.

Our approach here is balanced, on the positives with reclaiming and on the negatives that need recasting. It is also comprehensive. We naturally confront our past, in part and haphazardly, at events like weddings, funerals, holidays, and class reunions. All these events offer opportunities to reframe the lessons from our yesterdays. We experience them with varying degrees of awareness and rarely think of them as times to increase our self-knowledge, even though that often happens.

Here we are more intentional, as we systematically address the fundamentals that we all need to review. I will also encourage you to go past the basics into the specific memory sets that hold the most meaning for you. We will use both creative and analytical approaches, and you'll get to decide what is your best combination of thinking processes. Only our own higher-level thinking can address the three obstacles that our amnesia causes: not knowing who we are (identity), not using all of our gifts (potential), and not doing it our way (self-direction).

## WARNING ON TRAUMA

This book provides methods for attaining more self-awareness and wisdom. It is not a replacement for therapy. All of us have a range of negative experiences in our yesterdays, from the slightly negative to the horrific. If you have not done any work on the serious negative events, get some professional therapeutic help. Even if you have done some therapeutic work, but you still have some past events that bring up significant pain, anger, or anxiety, you need to take action. Also, if you suffer from intense mood swings, see a professional. Go to the sources in your network—a friend, the Internet, your church—and find referrals for the assistance you need.

I am not pushing you lightly on this. Can you feel that big heavy push in the middle of your back to take this step? That is me.

I used to be reluctant, as many of us still are, to use a therapist to review past problems and limits. I used to think therapy and its claim of healing damage incurred in earlier life chapters was for those who were not normal or strong enough to be happy.

I don't think that anymore.

---

**You may need a professional partner to extract the right meaning from your earlier suffering and wounds, to create a plan and the steps needed for healing, and to assure you that you can move ahead.**

---

The more we bury old damage by not attending to it, the greater the chances that we are seriously stuck somewhere in our lives and work, not knowing how to proceed. Bully bosses, wimpy workers, women who love too much, men who can't access their feelings, those who are afraid to assert or have to be the center of attention, everyone who borders on or is a full-fledged workaholic—all are stuck in past mental/emotional patterns that limit their life, work, and leadership.

So go get some competent therapy if you never have, and you can read more on this in chapter 5, on recasting.

⇨ *Core takeaway idea:* **Your yesterdays are filled with lessons and energy waiting to be tapped.**

## ▶ STATEMENTS OF INTENT TO ENGAGE THE WILL AND FIRE THE IMAGINATION

My past is a unique and extremely valuable resource.

I absorb the lessons of my personal history as a primary means to embrace my potential and to explore my future with a full appreciation of my gifts.

Yesterday's lessons are available to me as a storehouse of wisdom for today's decisions.

## ▶ QUESTIONS FOR SELF-REFLECTION

The executive mentioned at the outset was fired because of his false sense of self, born of the inflated judgment that his past had given him powers that set him above the team, including his boss. What haunts me is how we all carry around faulty thinking, the kind just out of our awareness, like in the old V8 Juice ads where people hit themselves on the head in a "What was I thinking?!" moment of realization. Our poor learning and unlearning, embedded in our history, inevitably leads to self-induced setbacks perhaps even more severe than getting fired.

Let's begin the process of lessening that unlearning with some questions concerning our self-awareness that deserve our attention.

- ▶ How well do I integrate the gifts of my body, my mind, my will, my feelings, my sense of play, my enthusiasm for learning, in a way that helps me to be a well-balanced person?
- ▶ Do I get stuck in a major way of being (I am my relationships, or I am my thoughts, or I am my work) and underdevelop the other ways of being?

▶ How well do I follow my own path versus the one that my family permitted or my surroundings rewarded?

▶ Do I combine the best of the models for life and work that I observed, and options I was given, with those I created for myself? What examples can I think of?

*So we beat on, boats against the current,*
*borne back ceaselessly into the past.*

—F. Scott Fitzgerald, *The Great Gatsby*

~~~~~~~~~~~~~~~~~~~~~~~~~~~~~~~~~~~~~~~~~~~~~~~~~~~

# PART I

## Discovering the Power of Your Past

PART I BEGINS a reorientation to our past by exploring why such a reorientation is necessary in the first place. We will look at why the past is such a strong current and what keeps us from tapping the power of going with, not against, the current.

We miss the possibility of deeper, generative decisions for our work and lives when our orientation to the identity-forming events from our yesterdays is largely forgotten. Our tendency with our past is to ignore, forget, and purposefully leave it unattended. *Amnesia* is the name we are giving to this collection of tendencies, not in the clinical sense, but as a metaphor for not tapping the power of our past.

Much has been written on how to plan for the future and how to stay in the now. Let's look at how to harness the power of your unique history by understanding why we don't and why we have to, which is explored in chapter 1, and how the dynamics of your yesterdays have such powerful carry-over to the present, which is discussed in chapter 2.

These are our first steps in recovering from our amnesia. Let's begin.

*The Past—the dark unfathom'd retrospect!*

*The teeming gulf—the sleepers and the shadows!*

*The past—the infinite greatness of the past!*

*For what is the present after all but a growth*
*out of the past?*

—WALT WHITMAN, "PASSAGE TO INDIA"

# Chapter One: The Underused Past: The Price of Forgotten Yesterdays

*The movie* Eternal Sunshine of the Spotless Mind *revolves around a clever variation on the amnesia theme. The central characters, played by Jim Carrey and Kate Winslet, willfully induce a partial amnesia to erase the painful memories of a relationship gone bad. It works but has mixed results. At one point, Carrey, sensing his memories disappearing, the good along with the bad, pleads with the doctor inducing the amnesia—"Pl-e-a-s-e, let me keep this memory, just this one!"*

*They are drawn to each other a second time, experiencing an unconscious attraction even with the conscious memories gone. Memories or no, even with spotless minds, their destinies are woven together as they get a second chance to go after love.*

*We are all those two characters. We have forgotten why we are pulled toward and pushed away from certain people and events. We attempt to have fresh, spotless minds when we move into our lifework, but a vague familiarity reminds us that we erase memories at our peril. Forgetting dooms us to repeating. We are destined to return to that which we must encounter until we fully absorb our core lessons.*

## Underusing the Past: The First Hurdle Is the Norm of Mediocrity

We all know that our yesterdays have value. When we hire someone with "lots of experience," what we want is the knowledge that comes from past experiences. We know that older people teach younger people and elders provide wisdom to later generations. Many of us seek mentors. But as useful and common as it is to use others' pasts at work and in life, it is just as common to neither truly understand nor fully value the power of our own yesterdays.

Because of this devaluating amnesia, we rarely attempt to fully harvest the rich lessons of our own lives. The common discounting, forgetting, underuse, and misuse of our past deprive us of our truest stories.

**With roots not anchored in the deep and fertile soil of our true identity, we don't know who we are, why we think the way we do, what gives us joy and repels us, or how to sow the seeds and harvest the fruit of our talents and dreams.**

With a half-complete history in mind, the level that the world around us accepts and promotes, we misjudge who we are, what we can do, and how to do it (identity, potential, and self-direction). Instead, we channel our talents into the narrow confines of what society offers us, such as the many jobs that are either too small or not designed for the people that fill them. Seeing minimal connection from formative times in youth and early work events to our current reality, we are left to the culture's advice. A misinformed boss, a columnist from *Rock-Hard Abs Forever Magazine*, and bloggers in love with their opinions are all happy to tell us what to do. This is the mediocre norm that we suffer without knowing it and which we have to escape if we want things large and soul-resonant to happen in our life.

We are trained to make this mistake: listen to the following statements about the past from a few 20th- and 21st-century sources, both pop and highbrow.

**If you delve into the past it will become a bottomless pit.**
—ECKHART TOLLE[1]

**I tell you the past is a bucket of ashes.**
**I tell you yesterday is a wind gone down,**
—CARL SANDBURG, "PRAIRIE"[2]

Is it any wonder that we don't think much of our past? Countless other statements about the past have this identical drift: get over it, don't think about your past. There is nothing really there to pay attention to. Don't waste your time.[3]

## MISJUDGING OUR HISTORY: OUR COMMON ERRORS

Here is a list of the common errors that prevent us from having an optimal relationship with our yesterdays for navigating our journey. Some are more obvious than others.

All are damaging. You get to be the judge of your favorite tactics and the degree of ballast and drag you absorbed on your journey. (You enjoyed some smooth sailing as well, of course, but here we are talking about our errors.)

## Underuse Mistakes

*Avoid/numb out:* When we don't explore the painful parts because they are negative.

"*I never go there.*"

*Ignore:* When we don't use the positive parts for their power to define, inform, and inspire.

"*Why think about that?*"

*Erase:* When we flat-out regress, forgetting what we once knew, and need a wake-up call that goes like

"*Wow, how did I get so out of touch with that part of me?*"

## Misuse Mistakes

*Pathologize:* Having a clinical view of our history, sucking the passion out of it, and giving it a dry, clinical diagnosis.

"*My mom was a basket case, perhaps even a borderline personality, and that is why I . . .* "

*Romanticize/sentimentalize:* Having a Pollyannaish, sanitized view of everything we encountered. This is often the result of our heads' opinion that to admit any suffering or heart pain is a sign of weakness, so we suppress.

"*You know, I can't think of a single downside to my perfect past.*"

*Demonize/victimize:* When the villains from our past take center stage and we stay helpless or unforgiving or otherwise stuck. If we emphasize the villains, it is demonizing:

"*The good-for-nothings set me back for a lifetime.*"

If we emphasize ourselves, it is victimizing: *"I wish I would have had the right family—who knows what I might have become."*

We all do some of the above. We have our own variations of these statements and many more particular ones, since our lives are singular and our brains are uniquely organized around the constellation of experiences and interpretations that are ours alone. The errors are both the sloppy habits that divert us and the protective mechanisms we put in play to help us understand the events we could not put into perspective at the time they happened. They become problems when we stick with the errors for the long term and don't claim our own truth.

## The Upshot: Yesterday's Lessons Lost

Most people make their idiosyncratic mix of mistakes because they don't assess their past as full of value anchors, energy sources, and practical lessons for how to work and live. Hardly anyone reviews his or her yesterdays systematically with a view toward growth. Our collective amnesia makes it so. Most people I encounter consider their personal history to be mixed and less than perfect. It is somewhere between "sorta good" and "sorta bad"—not useless, but not particularly useful either. (There are exceptions, of course, and they will show up throughout the book.) These people have decided that their less-than-ideal past, since it is over, has little more to teach them about making today's decisions for tomorrow's life chapters.

Wrong!

One Venezuelan-born entrepreneur I interviewed, Rosanna Figuera, who has an executive search and coaching business in Manhattan, talked about her former thinking: "I used to think the past should stay in the past . . . that the past was baggage." Some of us still think of our yesterdays in this negative mode. We may work on our self-awareness but are in the now-is-all-that-matters camp, intentionally ignoring our past.

Wrong!

Skimming over your rich life history with its challenges and resources is a major error. I see this skimming frequently. As a coach, I see people with big events in their yesterdays, perhaps a teacher who changed their life for the good, or an early boss whose negativity they fought to overcome. They barely acknowledge the event as worth revisiting and therefore miss the developmental significance of their own experience. This leaves them with blind spots for which they pay a price and unaware of how to proceed in accepting the tasks of their own growth.

Leaders and professionals busily attack their tasks but often fall short in the crucial act of extending their unique humanity, one based on a thorough knowledge of self, into their role. This is the identity problem at work. When I interview leaders' teams to give them actionable feedback, I often find that the leaders have only partially found their own voice. This lack of self-authorship stems from the leaders' not claiming the singular voice that is theirs to claim, the one that emerges from their unique history. These leaders can use the *Harvard Business Review* article they read on the way to the board retreat to get by in some instances. But such tactics won't work for the long term or in the real clinches, when character counts and a crisp leadership identity is the primary fallback asset.

The director of INSEAD's Global Leadership Centre, Manfred F. R. Kets de Vries, puts it this way: "Plenty of executives refuse to consider the possibility there may be issues in their work and life that originate in the area beyond . . . their immediate awareness."[4] In my work, I see large numbers of partially successful leaders suffering from this accepted blind spot of under-use and amnesia. I get to regularly view, close up and very personal, the enormous difference it makes to use our past well.

**Without knowledge of our past, we do not have a primary guiding light to help us walk creatively and bravely into our future. We won't make the changes we need to propel us into new and more enriching lifework.**

## SEEING THE ERRORS AT PLAY

The notion of making full use of our yesterdays is for people who care about best practices for their work and life, and who deeply desire to discover their most authentic and ever-emergent voice. They want more than to accept the hazy, lazy, mediocre middle of thinking about a life path that matters but not walking on that path.[5]

Perhaps the biggest reason why we settle for mediocrity is that we are used to seeing it. I have seen the mediocre middle in accessing the power of our yesterdays with hundreds, probably more like thousands, of people, both individually and in groups. Conversely, when we come across people whose work is a natural extension of their essence, we are drawn to their personal power and can even be moved by their presence. These self-defined people are ordinary, too, of course, and as humans they suffer from the usual feet of clay, but they have done their homework and know the power embedded in their yesterdays.

One reason we use to justify the amnesia and not work with our yesterdays is the well-known fact that we don't recall our yesterdays with accuracy. An extreme example is how some self-proclaimed victims of abuse eventually realize that they fabricated the stories that had become so real to them. So if our memories are faulty, why use them? Because most of us naturally review our memories and have a set of yesterdays we ponder. The past we have is as much or more about the interpretation of the events as it is about the events themselves. Our job, therefore, is to look at that interpretation, the "truth" upon which our belief systems have settled. Not to look at those "truths" is to reside in that mediocre middle.

### Avoid/Numb Out: *Not Exploring the Painful Parts*

This one is common. You hear it all the time, sometimes stated, "Let's not go there." Just as often, you hear numbing and avoiding between the lines, as in the anxious language of men when they make their jokes about "touchy-feely, kumbaya" moments at work.

A few years back, I had a remarkable interaction with a group of business owners. As I have done a few hundred times, I presented a topic to CEOs on personal and professional change. We gathered at the clubhouse of a golf course on a warm spring day. The stag energy in the group was powerful as the guys chortled and harrumphed, teased, and laced the morning's conversation with swearing and off-color jokes. I was in an element I knew well: men without women around and without the accompanying social constraints.

Their facilitator told me, in preparation for the meeting, that several of the men had been divorced in the past year. The following exchange occurred:

"I would rather pull out my fingernails one at a time than have my wife look at me and say, 'We need to have a talk.' Man, I hate that!" declared the handsome 40-year-old CEO on the outdoor deck of the clubhouse.

His buddy chimed in, "Yeah, I know what you mean. I especially hate it when she says it in the morning, and then I have to think about it al-l-l da-a-ay!!"

Groans of understanding and nods of empathy issued from most of the others. You could hear their collective yesterdays and the intimate conversations that petrified them clawing back to the surface of their awareness. Their numbing and avoiding tactics were only Band-Aids and could not work in the long term.

My job with this group became quickly apparent as I picked up the spirit of their sharing: to coax them into considering that, while their business lives were successful, their growing edge for happiness rested on the side of understanding intimacy and investing in relationships. They were lopsided executives, skilled professionally and financially, and underdeveloped in how to love. They barely allowed themselves to consider what they were missing.

We had a powerful exchange that day. Who knows what one day with them accomplished? But they had a permanent facilitator/coach for the group, the person who brought me in, so my hope was to let the wisdom of the group and the skill of this coach ease them into new heart space with these demanding women who had the audacity to want to "talk."

**Ignore:** *Not Using the Positives to Define and Inspire*

An error in learning from our yesterdays occurs when we become frozen in patterns that stunt growth by keeping us busy using only secondary gifts. This holds for all people, even those enjoying some worldly success. We all know people who are bored with work and locked into the paycheck, and this may be us now or not so long ago. To stay with work patterns that are "OK" but not an expression of an essential part of us is a slow poison. It may be imperceptible at first, but over time the ignoring becomes more toxic.

A colleague from my Omaha youth, Joe Vacanti, is an accountant. He rose to the top of his profession, training other accountants. But as the years went by, he began to suffer as he faced the same processes and the same crazy tax season. Like many a successful professional, Joe had gotten crispy around the edges from the routine of a career gone stale. He suffered from a common pattern—he had made a career decision at age 18 that he would have to live out for the next 40-plus years. For him, this work was not close enough to the parts of him that were theatrical and fun, that had liked to participate in the school plays and musicals.

Joe suffered well (yes, there is such a thing—see chapter 7). He stayed aware of the price, searching and experimenting without burdening others and complaining. While still connected to his profession today and not fully jettisoning his enormous quantitative-thinking gifts, he has moved into more creative work. He teaches in hospitals with a board game and works as an extra in movies, and feeds his soul with these pursuits and more that may come.

To ignore our essential gifts, the ones revealed to us in our yesterdays, is a slow slide into misery.

Our history is a source of our originality and creativity. When we act on it and don't ignore it, our history can enliven our career, even if it has gone as stale as yesterday's beer.

## Erase: *When We Flat-Out Go Backward, Forgetting What We Once Knew*

Not all misuses of our history are easy to read, however, and the subtle, trickier kinds are often the ones that hold us back the most, precisely because they sound so reasonable. It does not have to be a big outrageous falsehood that is limiting your life's work and ways to contribute; it can even be a lesson that you forgot and distorted.

### The Executive Who Turned from Learning to Telling

66 One of my favorite long-term clients has made a request: "We have this executive by the name of Bill, with this great track record for four years, but his stress level or something has him way off base, and he is annoying about everyone—his team and boss and customers, even his close supporters. Do you want to work with him for a while, John? Because if he keeps this up, he will get fired. And we think that is a last option, because we know he can do better—we have seen it."

I said yes—a formerly highly regarded exec who had become disruptive must have been doing it for a reason. So Bill and I began to work together.

In our conversations, I soon learned that Bill had run out of patience. While his career involved applying his considerable brilliance to fixing problems and getting work done, he had unofficially and compulsively appointed himself the fixer of everybody else's problems, which quickly gained him royal-pain-in-the-butt status. He had accelerated from never being shy about contributing, to badgering peers, his team, and even his boss. Bill had gotten some feedback that he had become obnoxious and unproductive, but a large amount of stress kept him from containing himself. Some of his investments were going very wrong, and the money for his kids' college tuition and his family's future was almost gone. He had not told anyone about this at work.

So Bill and I had several conversations, the kind that I have had with hundreds of other people doing less than their best, many of whom knew it. We worked on the stress and the communication patterns.

In our sessions, I took Bill to a few big lessons from his past. One lesson he recalled vividly from his early days at IBM was that he found something positive and things to learn everywhere, especially in his team's mistakes. He had formed this thinking as a positive catalyst for change and a steady leadership contribution. This was the lesson that he forgot and pushed aside in the stress of watching the kids' tuition dwindle. He had misinterpreted his past, turning "I use mistakes as a learning opportunity for the team" into "I see mistakes and single-handedly try to fix them with my solution." He threw in a little victimization for good measure—"Why am I surrounded by dummies who can't see the solutions?"

Within days, Bill was able to stop the intensity, and within a few weeks he had gotten back on track and regained his old ways. In his words, "I had become stuck as a know-it-all hijacker of meetings. . . . I was trying to help, and instead I was seeing stupidity everywhere and could not shut up."

What Bill had needed was a few deep and consistent reminders of who he wanted to be because of who he had been. He had used the lessons from early in his career well, but the stress of losing some of the family nest egg had turned his learning style into a know-it-all style. To prevent backsliding, we kept up the conversations over several months. Bill carried on well, with a few predictable slips, negotiating a number of important deals before he left the company 18 months later. He left on such positive terms that he did several more deals with his former company when he became COO of a startup and began to re-fund the family's future. 99

Stories like Bill's illustrate the positive power of yesterday and the harvest of errors that we reap when we erase the lessons of yesterday.[6]

### Pathologize: *To Have a Clinical View of Our Past That Sucks the Passion Out of Our Yesterdays*

Pop psychology has made us all amateurs in naming our inner dynamics—a good thing as general awareness of emotional intelligence expands, but not without its dangers. Sticking with clinical language is one such danger, as we can use it to hide from ourselves behind a wall of analytical diagnosis, versus engaging with the creativity and courage we need for our growth.

We all hear things like

- ▶ I'm naturally intuitive, and my P is off the charts, so you know what that means!
- ▶ I am so left-brained, and I am on this crazy right-brained team and they all drive me crazy.
- ▶ My feminine side is nonexistent, so buck up and take this feedback the way it comes—straight at you.
- ▶ I think I am projecting onto my boss stuff from my family—no wonder this feels more desperate than it is.

All of this language can be of use, but it can also get in the way, by giving our autonomy away to some useful theory that categorizes us. When we pathologize, we are failing to take responsibility for ourselves. We are being too glib and too cognitive about our past and its good and bad moments. We are creating an unhealthy distance from our experience, rather than confronting it and taking it to heart.

### Romanticize/Sentimentalize: *Pollyanna Moves to Sanitize and Minimize*

This error is especially socially acceptable. It sounds positive, creates no enemies or victims, and can be useful, like all the errors, to a point. When it goes past the point of seeing the good in our yesterdays, we can be camped out in our own la-la land.

---

**When we make up probable-sounding lies to ourselves about how good we had it, we sentimentalize the power of our past away, filling it with fictional knickknacks of no consequence.**

---

Many of us have a past filled with beautiful memories—mine is. And yet to push out the harsh or tough memories without confronting them as an adult is to become captive to our positive fictions. We do this not knowing any better and in hope of avoiding the effort and tears that may lie ahead in naming the truth, the sadness and the badness, of those episodes.

I have seen families frequently and goodheartedly recount and laugh about numerous alcohol-enhanced family events over a summer holiday, for instance, with outrageous stories and funny dialogue. I rarely hear those families tell stories of the damage they have endured with that same alcohol.

I have seen people refuse to name the negative impact of a really bad boss, not wanting to admit the damage incurred and the time it took to recover. The phrase "I am taking the time off to fully detox" comes from someone who understands that romanticizing and sentimentalizing will not serve him or her in the long term, even if minimizing sounds heroic at first.

### Demonize/Victimize: *Getting Frozen in Passivity*

We all have bad actors in our past, some of whom may have been advanced saboteurs who worked hard to limit our possibilities. More than the evil ones, the ignorant actors in your life tried their best and still managed to botch up your capabilities with untruths and judgments. And sometimes we are our own bad actors and did the damage to ourselves.

We have a job to do with the memories of the bad actors. First, don't minimize them. Second, let them go and move on. Demonizing is missing the second part.

Victimizing is often in concert with demonizing. In its blatant forms, it is easy to spot, as we use the past to rationalize who we are in the present. We have all heard something like this: "Well, my dad was a distant guy and worked all his life way too hard, so I am kind of emotionally distant myself. Always will be." Or, "I have always had this temper, and it runs in the family, so get over it."

Wrong!

Mining the past for strains of influence is useful; indeed, that is what we will do in part 2. We will do this work with great care, however. To attribute one of your current traits or patterns to your parents or a teacher, or to an event from your past, is excuse-making of the first order. It is a way-too-common abuse of the past, as bad as ignoring your yesterdays altogether with willful amnesia.

---

**What to do about the limits and tendencies we absorb from our past, including those stemming from the unfortunate things we had to endure, will be a part of our discussion. But we will make no excuses.**

---

The less blatant forms of victimizing can be just as damaging. I see leaders not owning the part they played in mistakes and divorced people not owning their part ("My wife didn't want to be married anymore—funny thing"). As Alfred Adler is purported to have said, "The life lie of the neurotic person is failure to accept personal responsibility." Victimizing ourselves in the interpretation of memories is a great way to live into life lies.

## Our Opportunity: Correct the Misrepresentations

*Be prepared to start thinking of your own past in new, creative ways. The past is there to help us if we want to use it. Energy infuses us and insight guides us when we harvest the life wisdom and motivational uplift available upon skillful reflection.*

I know the story of a woman who put up with an abusive husband for a long time. She would put icepacks in the refrigerator early on Friday nights, the most common nights for the abuse, for her use later that evening. Applying ice quickly really does limit the swelling—can you imagine that as a self-care strategy? She had an interpretation for this process: "He could not stop himself," she told herself, "but he loves me." This was her longstanding mental representation of the abuse.

Eventually she left her abuser. When asked why, she had a clear explanation. "I have never had coffee in my life. I am a tea drinker. One day he asked me if I wanted some coffee like he was asking a normal coffee drinker. He had never known I drink tea. He did not know me, pay attention to me, or love me." The coffee question, more than years of abuse, convinced her that her love explanation was not based on truth. She could then set herself free. Her mental representation, based on a sentimentalized interpretation, had kept her stuck and preparing icepacks for Friday nights.[7] While this may be an extreme example, we all have equivalent adaptations, substituting some less-than-optimal set of explanations and their accompanying behaviors for the real thing. These can be called our blind spots, our misaligned thoughts and behaviors, our addictions, or our stuck points. We hear them all the time:

- ▶ I have always been direct . . . too bad my people are so sensitive.
- ▶ My calendar is always full. I just miss appointments because I have so much to do.
- ▶ Deadlines are way too arbitrary. I do the work the way it is supposed to be done, and if I miss a few deadlines, the team can adapt.

Whatever we name them, past lessons poorly learned
are today's defended misrepresentations needing to be
exposed.

When we address these falsehoods, we begin to make
progress on the three shortfalls: we align with our true
identity, we activate our potential, and we write and live
our own script, not the ones we inherited.

*A clarifying point:* Don't be fooled that you are tapping
all the power of your yesterdays if you have some stories
you like to tell. One common type of underuse of the past is
getting stuck in our favorite stories and telling them repeat-
edly. We may be on our way to becoming the midlifer who
has stories we find reasons to regularly tell, to anyone within
earshot. When we do this, we may well be unhealthily reminiscing, refusing to live into our future and using predomi-
nantly our old anchors for meaning. A rich set of stories told
or recalled at the right time is priceless. But beware of the
underuse of the past that is disguised as story-born wisdom.
The phrase that tips you off to this reminiscent stagnation
is, "That reminds me of the time . . ."

Be prepared to rework some of these old stories for new
lessons—that will be one of our approaches.

### THE COLLECTIVE PRICE: THE EMPTINESS OF LESSER PURSUITS

Many have observed that humanity has a persistent tendency to fall short, sometimes ridiculously short, of its
potential. Lots of images describe this shortfall. One of my
teachers used to say that we are all dressed up with nowhere

to go. Carl Jung said that we are wearing shoes that are too small. This observation provides the basic background for our discussion on our yesterdays. An enriched set of practices about our yesterdays can shift us toward fuller use of our gifts and energy, expanding those small shoes bound to give us psychological and career bunions, while generating the inner fulfillment that comes from good work and the right fit.

Many a thinker has created his list for why the human family stays well below the creativity and good of which we are capable. But the basic fact remains that we too often choose to listen to our lesser angels, deny the best parts of our nature, and take the low road of passivity, dependency, and cheap thrills.

When I confront a list of the endless addictions and escapes that we use in our pursuit of the trivial, I get depressed. So let's avoid the list and admit the fact.

The massive pursuit of the trivial could well be our biggest moral failing. Strangely enough, we seem to be the species that has the audacity to bore God by directing our energy toward petty pleasures and silly gains.

The collective price for this false quest is the lack of social imagination and effort to create a better society. We have lots of stuff but not a society investing in its social capital. The individual price is a life of varying degrees of draining anxiety. We have endless entertainment choices, and complain about not having enough time and about too little meaning in our day-to-day lives. Anxiety is our friend when we confront it with courage. It is our nemesis when we try to escape it through a trip to the mall or the refrigerator, one more Facebook plunge we don't need, or reruns of *Law and Order* and NFL games from 2006. (OK, I had to include a little list after all.)

The pursuit of titillation is the easy pursuit, unworthy of us. It is on the outside. The pursuit of extensive self-knowledge is the difficult pursuit, worthy of our every effort, mistakes and all. It is on the inside. To know who we are by paying full attention to where we came from serves our worthiest pursuit—the expression of our best and deepest self.

▶**SUMMARY**

Without a set of informing stories from earlier in life and work, we have less of our future to create. We shortchange our path to our destiny and our contribution, allowing the culture into which we happen to be born to "wither the soft tissues of [our] soul," as Pat Conroy puts it in *The Prince of Tides*.[8] We have stored too little self-knowledge to counter the inertia and impact of the world.

**With an incomplete sense of our history, we miss the raw material we need to forge the work and career that is ours alone to create.**

The hurdles created by this amnesia-induced, wrong relationship with our yesterdays are big ones, because they are so accepted. We miss the gems and lessons that ignite our imagination, help define us, and provide us with our best energy for a lasting contribution. With demonizing and numbing and the other poor approaches, we stay confined by earlier events and draw conclusions that cloud our thinking, thwart our options, and limit our horizons for putting our gifts to use.

Let's look at how to capture the truth of your past in the next section. Let's put the power of your yesterdays to work for your highest efforts.

▷ *Core takeaway idea*: **Your yesterdays are filled with lessons and energy waiting to be tapped.**

### ▶ STATEMENTS OF INTENT TO ENGAGE THE WILL AND FIRE THE IMAGINATION

My best life and work efforts are the positive extensions of understanding and absorbing my unique history.

The lessons of my past are uniquely mine to own and express in my life's work.

I spring beyond the limits of my upbringing and my culture to live the deepest possibilities of my life.

### ▶ EXERCISES

#### Reflect on Your Favorite Mistakes

We all tend to repeat some mistakes about our yesterdays more than others. If you haven't already done so, make an educated guess about what your patterns are. But let's first take the positives:

▶ How do you use your past well? What are some examples?

▶ Which of the six errors of underuse and misuse do you tend to make the most—avoid/numb out, ignore, erase, pathologize, romanticize/sentimentalize, or demonize/victimize? What makes you think that?

### Reconsider One of Your Old Stories

The past may be irrevocable, a feature that gives it much power, But it is, curiously enough, not final. It is no more frozen than you are. As you revisit it again and again, you can find new lessons, draw new conclusions, be more blunt about the forces at play, or be more compassionate than you have ever been.

Think of one of your favorite stories from the past—with a teacher, a friend, a coach, a boss, or a project. Use the stories and examples provided thus far—Tommy Emmanuel and Chet Atkins, "I feel like a puddle"—as examples to get you going if needed.

Play your story over in your mind yet again, but slowly this time. Go past the headlines you often normally use, when you tell a short version of this story. Here are a few ways to help keep you from getting stuck in an old story and instead revivify it, and you in the process, by remembering it anew:

Tell a longer version to your spouse or a friend who has heard the story. Stop early on, as the story begins. What new facts can you bring in about you or about the context of the story?

What new feelings?

What about the back story can be elaborated on? What about the forces at play and the moving parts and people?

What new conclusions can you speculate on?

Record in a journal what new lessons and insights came your way, or what old ones sank a little deeper into your heart and mind.

*The past is never dead. It's not even past.*

—William Faulkner, Requiem for a Nun

## Chapter Two: Good and Bad News: Evoked and Compressed

*In Dickens's classic* A Tale of Two Cities, *just prior to the French Revolution, the aging Doctor Manette is withering from the many years of deprivation of an unjustified imprisonment in the infamous Bastille. He loses almost all of his memory and becomes a shadow of his former self. He hardly knows who he is and has forgotten his place in society. His only activity is to cobble shoes in the dark, a pastime to help him endure prison, and he can barely tolerate the light of day.*

*His family finds him and frees him, brings him home, and wonders what is possible for this shadow of a person. Manette's daughter, Lucie, asks him to reengage his will for his own betterment: "I hope," she says, yearning for the father she once knew, "you care to be recalled to life?" Manette answers haltingly, "I can't say."*

*Like Doctor Manette, how can we say, here at the beginning, if recalling our memories is a process from which we can gain? Let's begin by understanding the important lessons we forget with unattended memories.*

### Evoked and Enabled, Narrowed and Compressed

*You were not dropped into paradise when you were born. You encountered a world filled with the good, the neutral, the bad, the ugly, the funny, the tragic, the tender, the gritty.*

A ND THE WORLD acted on us, of course. While we are molded by this world, certain potentials are nurtured and called forth—we call this *evocation*; and other parts and talents are withered and stymied—we call this *compression*. Some of us are luckier in this many year encounter with the world than others—that is easy to observe. All of us, no matter what our stories as we encounter non-paradise, are responsible for knowing what we were born with as best as we can tell, what was nurtured and expanded, and what was muffled or limited.

After we grasp the importance of this decades-in-the-making process, we must find ways to

▸ limit and override the compressions, and
▸ own the power of the evocations that define us.

This is the recapturing and delimiting work we start in this chapter to fully define ourselves, use our potential, and set our own direction. We work against the amnesia that has served us to this point with mixed results.

Evocation is the calling forth and expansion of gifts and possibilities. Both the people and circumstances that surround us can draw out what and who we are, for the good of ourselves and the world. We discover our gifts and eventually form our voice in the world, largely through mentors, teachers, parents, coaches, bosses, and such institutions as churches; or through peers, cool siblings, and the school band. When these people and settings do their best to "educate" in the root sense of the Latin—*e(x) ducere*, which means "to draw out"—then evocations, hundreds of them in a lifetime, happen.

Compression is forceful containment: the squelching, muting, and stunting of these gifts and inner possibilities. Dark surroundings and missing props—a neighborhood with ugly prejudices, an absence of models for learning, an unthinking career counselor, a boss with an advanced sinister streak, a minister with a control problem—can all do their damage. Our gifts stay undiscovered, we make our living through secondary skills, or we channel our now-mangled energies toward money and other shallow ego substitutes for life when the compressions keep their grip. These also happen by the hundreds.

Wordsworth's famous lines in the poem "Ode: Intimations of Immortality" (1815) capture the essence of this cultural compression. He penned it before the fields of psychology and sociology were born, so it has the raw power of art before science. In the poem, he refers to youth as "Nature's Priest" because he has yet to experience social contamination:

> *Heaven lies about us in our infancy!*
> *Shades of the prison-house begin to close*
> *Upon the growing Boy,*
> *But He beholds the light, and whence it flows,*
> *He sees it in his joy;*
> *The Youth, who daily farther from the East*
> *Must travel, still is Nature's Priest,*
> *And by the vision splendid*
> *Is on his way attended . . .*

But when the youth becomes a man, the beams of heaven
and its possibilities have dimmed:

> *At length the Man perceives it die away,*
> *And fade into the light of common day.*[1]

Wordsworth describes the dark side of the compression,
a prison house of the mind slowly casting bigger and darker
shadows. We are unstamped and all potential in infancy.
But soon after birth, life and the circumstances we were
born into begin to channel and evoke that potential into
what the society knows, and to compress and snuff out
what it does not value.

The channeling cannot be prevented, nor should it be.
We live in space and time and in cultures that shape us for
our survival and much to the good.

**Nevertheless, all socialization is a narrowing of who you
are, and so there is a sadness about it. While parts of you
are growing, you lose other parts, and still other parts get
distorted and narrowed and channeled.**

The following model describes what happens to the pure
potential of the infant as it gets channeled and shaped by
life. With the whole potential of the baby at the top, by the
time life happens, some parts, or pieces of the puzzle, survive and some parts get left out (see bottom of the funnel).

The compression starts rather early, by our second or
third breath. In a *New Yorker* cartoon, the starry-eyed new
parents gaze lovingly at their little newborn in its crib, and

**CULTURAL COMPRESSION**

the mommy lovingly declares, "Oh, it's a manager!" She was looking down the funnel ahead to the outcome she would be proud of (see image below).

The neuroscience of this formative process is, of course, that neural pathways are created by these early circumstances. Children born into poverty, struggling families, and faulty schools have different prospects for their brain development than those born into enriching surroundings.

**CULTURAL COMPRESSION**

Art and science come at this reality in their own ways, and my approach is more through the artists' viewpoint.

Another artistic allusion, from playwright Eugene O'Neill, comes more than a century after Wordsworth. In *Long Day's Journey into Night*, Mary, the mother, declares,

**None of us can help the things life has done to us. They're done before you realize it, and once they're done they make you do other things until at last everything comes between you and what you'd like to be, and you've lost your true self forever.**[2]

I have more hope than either O'Neill or Wordsworth, because they both ignore the evocation process. Still, cultural compression is a mega-fact that we must all confront. We must accept the shrinking of big and good parts of us as an inevitability, as sad and even bitter as that can be, because it explains so much.

Our culturally enabled amnesia sets in precisely at this profound truth. We forget, for the most part, how we are shaped through evoking and compressing. Unless we work at it, we cannot know how to regain those gifts that are naturally ours and those that must be unearthed, polished, and reclaimed.

Many of us, me included even well into the second half of my life, do not want to make any such admission about cultural compression. I concluded (romanticizing was one of my tactics) that my choices were more at play than they were, and that early life and early adult compressions were minor. I did not know that I had amnesia and thought I could will myself ahead by setting goals and sticking to them.[3]

Goal setting works, of course, but not always. When a compressed and forgotten part of us is not working in concert with the part of us that set the goal, the goals are often short of our best choices, or we don't reach them. Many 20-somethings feel the acute dissonance of their unaligned parts as they launch into adulthood. Forty-somethings may have similar feelings, but in Wordsworthian terms the prison house has had the time to cast a longer shadow by this decade and numbing may mute the dissonance (unless it is time to act out in a midlife crisis). If any-age person has gone up some rungs on a career ladder, he may not want to know, in Joseph Campbell's famous phrase, that the ladder is leaning against the wrong wall.

I had to really work to understand the power of cultural compression in my life and work, and you may have to as well. In my case, I had to confront the power of compression and its long-lasting effects. I could not avoid repeating some of my past patterns, no matter how much I willed and tried to talk myself into new alternatives. In my work, as an example, when I more fully faced the truth of my yesterdays, I stopped working so hard on others' good projects and started focusing on my own original contributions. (More on this example later).

Some version of denial, or overemphasizing only a part of the process of compression, is what creates much of our less-than-healthy relationship with our past. The following chart is a guide to help you consider what your tendency may be.

As adults on the other side of our big, formative evocations and compressions, we need (our work is) to go back and see what we need to regain and what we want to get rid of. Otherwise, we find ourselves in work and lives that we only partially chose at best, ones that we were primarily compressed into. This recapturing/delimiting task often constitutes one of the relatively short but crucial beginning segments of my coaching and mentoring work.

## OUR TENDENCIES WITH EVOCATIONS AND COMPRESSIONS

| FOUR MISTAKES MADE WITH BOTH COMPRESSIONS AND EVOCATIONS | ASSOCIATED MISTAKE WITH OUR YESTERDAYS | HOW WE JUSTIFY THEM |
| --- | --- | --- |
| 1. To not admit compression is to pretend. | Romanticize and numb. | I had no downers of any significance whatsoever. |
| 2. To only admit compression is to blame. | Victimize and demonize. | My life would be so different if I had not had all those weird folks around. |
| 3. To not admit evocation is to deny. | Ignore and forget. | I am self-made . . . I can't think of anyone or anything that powerful for me. |
| 4. To only admit evocation is to go Pollyanna. | Sentimentalize. | I had the best mentors and parents and teachers. It's all good. |

I start by being curious about how my clients encountered the world in which they started, at home, school, and work. I can view their current state of inner challenge—always accompanied on the outside by a daunting set of leadership challenges—from the capabilities and awareness they formed in their yesterdays. I want to know my clients' inner theater as they go about their tasks. That way, I can help replace the scripts that don't serve them fully with better ones more aligned with who they are and want to be as leaders.

We end up with our deepest thought patterns, the operating instructions for our minds, through compression and evocation. This is why yesterday has such power. It is why the committee of voices in your head can take you nowhere.

## Limiting Thoughts: Well-Disguised, Faulty Operating Instructions

We all drag around belief patterns from our past, some of which, if they ever worked at all, are now blocking our options. These patterns have little to do with reality and engender self-limiting thoughts and actions that we often don't recognize as negative, and that hamper our imagination and even our courage when and where we need them most.

How many times have you found yourself in a mental funk/stuck-if-I-do-stuck-if-I-don't polarized dilemma? You feel out of workable options, and you are left with choices and thoughts like these:

- ▶ I just hate giving presentations, so I have to give up this opportunity.
- ▶ I am a working fiend. I can really put in the hours. Maybe I will get a social life one day.
- ▶ I am a quiet type, and sometimes this leads to others' taking advantage of me—well, pretty often, actually.
- ▶ I can stay in this stupid job another year, getting by. I need the money and don't have to think about it.

## *The Executive That Nobody Knew*

While I was coaching an executive with a ton of management know-how and limited leadership presence, the board and the employees, whom I interviewed as part of the engagement, all told me the same thing: "This guy is so private, we don't know anything about him and he won't share anything."

This was not his biggest issue, but it was tied to a lot of challenges he had as a leader. When I asked him what was important about being non-self-disclosing, he asserted that he came from a home with alcohol damage, "so I draw a very distinct line between my personal and professional life." We talked about that conclusion. When I challenged him that it was less like a line and more like a wall for those who worked with him, he started to reconsider and made small steps to change his interactions.

Still, he remained stilted, task-oriented to a fault for a leader responsible for the atmosphere of the office, and he was extremely reluctant to give up whatever conclusions those early lessons taught him.

Not all my stories have happy endings.

These kinds of assertions, always with at least the possibility of some truth, are the kind of everyday self-talk, *born somewhere in your compressed past*, that stifles your imagination and choices, preventing you from moving into your best self. Statements like the above reveal limiting mental maps and models. They stay with us for so long and operate so automatically that they disappear from our awareness. They create the fish-not-knowing-it's-in-the-water problem of major magnitude—it is so very hard to see what you are habitually acclimated to.

Our minds struggle to slow down enough to observe our conscious thoughts—those sounds and pictures and feelings that get projected onto our inner mental screen. This what-is-on-my-screen level is where we find the list of limiting thoughts above, like "I can stay in this stupid job" or "I hate giving presentations." About 100 years ago, artists like James Joyce were showing the world how this level of thinking works, and psychology started probing beneath this surface.

**The mind struggles even more to become aware of our thoughts at a deeper level, the operating-system level of consciousness mainly out of our awareness.**

**These work much less visibly below the user-interface/on-my-screen level and are the thoughts behind the thoughts, the ones started with evocations and compressions.**

The operating-system-level thoughts stay mostly unspoken, draw little attention to themselves, and get disguised as useful guideposts, even as they lead to silly choices and destructive habits: "I can stay in this stupid job (on-my-screen level) because I am used to getting by, since work is mainly something to grind out and endure (less-detectable thought behind the thought)."

To live and work more fully, you must detect, unmask, and expose these hidden and forgotten patterns for what they are and how they affect you. One effective way to delimit our thoughts, the ones at the foundations of how we show up in work and life, is to systematically review how they got there. We don't begin to harvest the full power of our yesterdays until we unmask the deeper thoughts that started with our compressions.

We must each look again at what we thought we knew about ourselves, not that we have been mainly wrong, though that is a possibility, but primarily because there is more. This is the way to get rid of the quirky collection of self-limiting and exaggerated thought patterns, ones that are unique to each of us and sit happily and undetected alongside the robust and life-enhancing patterns.

## Choosing a Truthful, Balanced Interpretation

Going back to the list of self-limiting, on-my-screen-level thoughts, let's add the possible past events that got us to the faulty operating-system-level conclusions.

> ▶ I just hate giving presentations, so I have to give up this opportunity.
> *Early in my career, I blew a big presentation, froze up for a while, and lost it, totally, and now I suck at presentations.*

> ▶ I am a working fiend. I can really put in the hours. Maybe I will get a social life one day.
> *In school and early in my career, when I worked harder, I got the most praise. This is me, Mr. Endless Hours.*

> ▶ I am a quiet type, and sometimes this leads to others taking advantage of me—well, pretty often, actually —as they don't know what I want.
> *My third-grade friends used to laugh at the lisp I have grown out of, so I remain naturally quiet.*

▶ I can stay in this stupid job another year, getting by. I need the money.

*My first rough and tumble boss, who I really liked, would dole out his career advice: "An ugly buzzard in the hand is better than a peacock in the bush." Then he'd laugh and we'd all laugh with him. I think now that that is how he tried to keep us on his team.*

These thought-forming formulas behind the on-my-screen thoughts are the juicy ones. They come from our yesterdays, lurking in less-detectable forms than our normal thoughts, and they need to be reworked in order for us to overcome the unique version of compression that we each endured, and to fully embrace the unique evocations that made us.

Here it is in a nutshell (see next page).

## AN EXAMPLE: THE PROFESSOR SPRUNG FROM SECRETARIAL SCHOOL

Let's look at one life and how this works. This is the most extended example we will take, as it is so illustrative and multidimensional.

André Delbecq is a business professor at Santa Clara University, the former dean of the business school, and a mentor and guide to many. Every time André offers a course on spirituality in business, it fills up with working professional MBAs, the emergent high-tech leaders from all the faiths and religions that populate Silicon Valley. It is also often audited by senior executives. The course is one expression of his transformational work as an academic who has combined his knowledge of business with matters of the spirit.

## LEVELS OF THINKING: THE THOUGHTS BEHIND OUR THOUGHTS

| OUR THOUGHTS | HOW WE EXPERIENCE THEM | IMPLICATIONS FOR OUR WORK AND LIFE |
|---|---|---|
| **Level 1** Surface thoughts that come up on my mental screen. | Stream of consciousness/ flow of thoughts. | Occupy us with a steady stream of thoughts, some useful and others not. |
| | Everyday experience of our thought screen. | Images linked together based on external stimuli and run-on thoughts not chosen. |
| **Level 2** Deeper operating-system thoughts determined by our compressions and evocations. | Forgotten through amnesia, disguised as the committee of voices in our heads, whispering almost undetectable instructions. | Hidden and powerful; drive what we allow ourselves to consider at Level 1. |
| | Experience this level through reflection: thinking about our thinking. | Exercise our freedom when we replace the thoughts that haphazardly landed there with ones we choose as our own guides. |

As he relates the facts about his youth in Toledo and his life after that, you'll see my comments in parentheses. Notice the truth he tells about both the compressing and evoking events he experienced.

66 I was stricken with polio when I was between the eighth grade and high school and was confined to bed for long periods. [It took me] a year and a half to learn to walk, and I think without the Carnegie library I don't know what would have happened to me. A neighbor at Carnegie library provided me, during that time of recovery and long illness, an even more intense period of reading, and my aunt wisely gave me a book called *The Wisdom of China and India*, and it invited me into the spiritual and philosophical traditions of Taoism, Confucianism, Buddhism, and Hinduism. *(Evocation through reading and support.)* It was pretty heavy stuff for a 13-year-old. . . . It opened my mind to a great sense of knowledge as a source of creativity. . . . I went to work in factories, and because of polio I just wasn't strong enough; I would come home at night—I'd be in such pain I couldn't get out of the car—and stagger into the house after I rested in the car for three or four hours. And finally I realized I just couldn't do that kind of heavy factory work. *(Overcoming a blatant compression.)* And so I went into secretarial college *(not a full evocation for his bright mind, by any means, but a step in the right direction)* and learned typing and shorthand. I was from a French immigrant family where none of the members had gone to college. 99

From the confinement of polio and family not formally educated, to exhausting factory work, to secretarial school and shorthand—not necessarily a flourishing start for an academic with a business and spiritual bent. At the time André was encountering his world, he, like all of us, was partially aware, at best, of what was happening to him. It was only upon reviewing his past often, with imagination and honesty, that he became acutely aware.

He goes on to describe the evoking dimensions of young adulthood, in addition to the Carnegie library, from his Toledo past. Non-paradise (no, it is not the best of all possible worlds) is not done when you turn 17.

66 After secretarial school, it wasn't long before I became the administrative assistant to the director of residence at the University of Toledo and then the administrative assistant to the director of Catholic Social Services. And in each case, I became the personal assistant to a talented administrator. So I interned at a very early age in a confidential way to two very gifted administrators. 99

Here we must take note of the often-overlooked positive power of yesterday. Toledo was not all factories and polio and shorthand lessons. André endured Wordsworth's shades of the prison house, *and* he was nurtured and evoked by the Carnegie library and through apprenticing with competent administrator models. He used these as the growth influences for long-term lessons and guiding anchors of energy. He was both compressed and evoked by the world he encountered in Toledo. As all of us are required to do in youth, he took the beginning steps to discover and develop his native talents and gifts. André was creating his path, and it was being created for him.

In André's adult years, with the wisdom that comes with reflection, he kept refining his thinking about his Toledo-based launch. He got an advanced degree at the University of Indiana, which he chose because it requires no second language, an advantage because of his dyslexia. He took a faculty position at the University of Toledo. In doing so, he sloughed off a potential compression, witheringly delivered bad advice from a well-meaning mentor. "The opinion by a mentor that I should definitely not go to the University of Toledo really hurt," he says, "because he predicted my failure." André turned down offers from the likes of Carnegie Mellon. But at the University of Toledo, he got to experience breadth, which a bigger school with more specialties could not have fostered.

Throughout his life, André practiced self-reflection. He decided to do what is familiar to those who know the Jesuits—the Ignatian exercises, 30 days of guided spiritual reflection on the essence of Christ's impact on one's life.[4]

> 66 When I began my work in work-based spirituality, one of the great exercises within the spiritual exercises of St. Ignatius is to go slowly, and ponder slowly over each period of life, including the periods of great difficulty. And I probably spent two days doing that *(thinking about this thinking to choose his own conclusions)* . . . and it provided a profound sense of sources of support, even in difficult times. . . . Through all of this deep consciousness work I see that I am a product of my past, and my past is largely not of my making. 99

Being ahead of his time, André got more withering judgments from his peers about his move to combine business and spirituality:

> 66 When I went into spirituality *(André was way ahead of the curve)*, several people who were fellows of the Academy of Management said, "We don't believe spirituality belongs in a scientific

business school, and I'm sorry but you're no longer part of our group." They literally would not sit next to me. I was physically shunned by all the senior people in the Academy of Management. The unanimous decision of my colleagues [at Santa Clara] not to approve the course was borne heavily, and their continued unwillingness to approve the course for six years of struggle . . . that was tough.[5] 🙶

André persisted, used his innate sense of self-direction, and sloughed off the bad treatment and advice as he had done earlier. Capturing the power of his yesterdays has helped André to choose the operating-system-level lessons he needs to design his work. He remembered and drew strength and inspiration from the early days with the spiritual books and the administrators who were unflappable. The outcome has been a deep and lasting impact on many, for whom the world of commerce can be an exercise in applying spiritual principles. His calling, sprouted in his past and given life by his willingness to revisit it, has helped so many live their own.

## MISSING THE EVOCATIONS AND COMPRESSIONS

At many of the workshops I conduct, the participants tell their personal and professional history through a simple life-line exercise that you may well have done at some point. To get the exercise started, I show them a 20-year segment of my late adolescent and early adult life in graphic form on a flip chart.

The line that gets drawn looks like the image at the top of the next page.

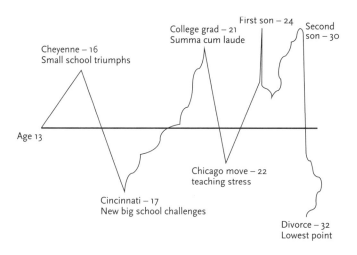

*One thing to notice:* I deliberately go below the midline on three occasions to describe what I learned from difficult times (see depression at 17 upon moving as an adolescent and a sad divorce at age 32, as two of the three). I don't want the participants to dwell exclusively on their tough chapters, but I do want them to balance out the above-the-line times with the compression times. Otherwise, we have a persistent tendency to list only the positives and evocations, and we even underestimate many of those. This makes for vanilla-flavored, bland life histories. It underestimates their power. It turns our destiny quest, no matter how average many aspects of it indeed are, into a bad sitcom with predictable lines.

**Avoiding the below-the-line struggles prevents us from owning the bare-knuckle truths that come from hardships. Underestimating the bad times and compressions mutes our passion and intensity.**

I ask the participants to draw a similar graphic line up to the present day for their life and leadership journey. Invariably, the graph that emerges shows the ups and downs depicting different career and life events and periods, not unlike mine, but with their own combination of good and bad plateaus, steep drops or gentle slopes of loss, and steady climbs of the good times.

When they are done, I have them tell the small group an abbreviated story of their life and leadership lessons learned up until the present. This basic life-line reflection never fails to be a powerful process of connection for the group (the primary reason I use it in team exercises) as they listen to others' stories, even if they have been working together for years. If I do this exercise with a work team, they are always stunned at how little they knew each other. Typically, they have never heard things like

> ► the broken careers that teammates have pieced back together—"after my three years of not working, except bagging groceries";
> ► the past victories and wonderful mentors—"Peter Drucker took the time to give me his best advice on several occasions";
> ► the tragedies and compressions they have endured— "I took care of my older brother after school for eight years of high school and college and never got to do any extracurricular activities."

I have heard all of the above and more, always an unpredictable combination of grueling trials and outrageously good fortune that hit in sequence.

During this exercise, it is very common to hear the ignoring of unclaimed yesterdays—"I had a normal childhood, school was OK, and my career start was uneventful"—and then they move into their current company as if their life started at age 30. They skip over their yesterdays as if family life, school, playing in the band, and a launch into a career are banal generalities, not singular adventures. They think that not much really happened because they don't have an eye trained for the everyday evocative miracles of their own development or for the deeper story that is always at play, trying to reveal itself to us.

A 40-something will often say, "Boy, until we did this lifeline exercise, I hadn't thought about that great boss I had in my mid-20s at Acme Cleaning Services—she pretty much molded me into the kind of boss I am today, I guess."

This is our amnesia. This is the ignore/avoid/numb error. Not only are we shamed away from the useless past ("I rarely think of my past and have little use for it"), but also we are busy with our work and children and grandchildren and community commitments. And there is the latest rerun of *CSI: Buffalo* to watch, video games to master, Facebook to update, kids or grandkids to haul to this week's soccer games, and all the other things that make up a day. Even a little sleep thrown in is helpful to most of us.

This lack of reflection—the tendency that makes the power of yesterday a well-kept secret and a damaging cultural blind spot—leads us to the mediocre middle that we must release if we want to harness our core and create work sizzling with soul.

## ▶ SUMMARY

Because we are functioning adults, we are under the misimpression that we have chosen most of our current thoughts. Yes, we have chosen some of them. And we let just as many, or more, slip into our minds as the thoughts behind our thoughts. As kids, we were in good and not-so-good environments. As adolescents, we endured the unhealthy and enjoyed the healthy adults and forces at play. As young adults in early jobs and life structures, we kept stumbling into the "shades of the prison house," the evocations and compressions that only early career work, early relationships, and extended educational commitments can bring.

With evoking and compressing happening to all of us from birth to death, we can understand why regular reflection is necessary. The way to escape any self-imposed or situation-imposed limits is to have dialogue with ourselves about what we took from our life events and what they mean for us now. We have to talk sense to ourselves, which is not easy to do, as simple as it sounds.

In spite of how your earlier life and work may have stymied and squelched some of your gifts and talents, the world really does want and need the best that you have to offer.

By reconsidering your yesterdays, you give yourself the chance to harness the power of self-knowledge at new levels. The way to move into a life and career that are truer expressions of you is to recognize which of your beliefs and choices, at the thought-behind-the-thoughts level, hold you back because they are only partially true and because they only partially work. Such recognition and rehabiting takes reflection, the kind in which I will be asking you to engage in the next section.

▷ *Core takeaway idea:* **Our yesterdays live on through the good and bad lessons we absorbed before we could choose our interpretations. Now we can choose.**

## ▶ Statements of Intent to Engage the Will and Fire the Imagination

My life is a learning laboratory filled with opportunities to live both fully and joyfully.

I embrace my past and all those people and places that have influenced it as the necessary steps for moving ahead into my essential work.

I create a dynamic and fruitful balance of both heartfelt acceptance for life's positive influences and gutsy rejection of the negative ones.

## ▶ Questions to Ask as You Reflect on Your Yesterdays

When I asked my friend and mentor Peter Block, the genius rabble-rouser, about his past, he said, "I had parents who loved me and I was born white. I won the lottery."

How would you say you did in life's lottery?

Or if the lottery question is not right for you, how would you describe your past?

To prepare for what is coming next, take a dive into the yes/no questions below. (They are yes/no to add an edge— you can ask open-ended versions of them.) Go where the

juice is for you. As always, these questions are just start-
ers—make up the ones that are most important for you.
They concern some of the major social structures that compressed and evoked you, one way or another.

▶ Do I fit into the family as a caretaker, a rebel, a stu-
dious one, a pillar of responsibility, or a source of
energy and fun, or don't I fit at all well in this family?

▶ Did I get into good schools and get a solid foundation for learning, or were the schools mediocre at
best, and I was bored or ignored by teachers and
therefore self-taught, with a lot of gaps where I could
use knowledge?

▶ Do I accept the gifts and limits of my gender and
explore what it means to say that I am a man or a
woman, or do I get stuck in a shallow, stereotyped
version of my gender and work too much on, say, my
physical beauty or capacity to win?

▶ Did I receive spiritual development that propelled me
into a life with spiritual imagination and the quest
for soul in the world, or did I get shortchanged with
moralistic religion or super-rational surroundings
where spiritual mystery was lost?

▶ Did my early bosses and work structures foster creativity, compliance, a herd mentality, my individuality, good disciplines, or bad disciplines like rewarding
for overwork and cutting ethical corners?

For all of the above, the question that might follow is:
How do you know?

*One must always maintain one's connection*
*to the past and yet ceaselessly pull away from it.*
*To remain in touch with the past requires*
*a love of memory. To remain in touch with*
*the past requires a constant imaginative effort.*

—Gaston Bachelard, *A Poetics of Fire*

~~~~~~~~~~~~~~~~~~~~~~~~~~~~~~~~~~~~~~~~~~~~~~~~~

# PART II

## Tapping the Power of Your Past

O UR LIVES FALL short and our shoes get too small
when we lack insight or fortitude. We don't do
the work we were meant for, because of a lack of imagination or courage, or both. I am not referring here to
the thought-based brainstorming kind of imagination
we use to generate ideas. There is a higher kind of
imagination.

**Soul-connected images and feelings can inspire us**
**when we link future possibilities with our deeply**
**engendered values and our uniquely lived histories.**

This is the deeper form of imagination connected to our deepest yearning and life dream. Our quest is less about brainstorm-rich plans and more about tapping core sources of will and power. Imagination of this type is a source for fostering human possibility. The images we carry in our memories, when viewed with eyes that are more focused on truth and potential than on facts, can be a source for inspiration and self-definition.

In this section, we use a three-step process—recall, reclaim, recast—to both analyze and imagine, the two sources for clear thinking and creatively powering up the will.

*And the past lives coiled in the present, beyond sight, beyond revocation, lifting us up or weighting us down, sealed away—almost completely—behind walls of pearl.*

—DAVID QUAMMEN, THE FLIGHT OF THE IGUANA:
A SIDELONG VIEW OF SCIENCE AND NATURE

# Chapter Three: **Recall**

---

*In the Japanese film* After Life, *a social-service office in heaven helps to prepare the newly dead for the after-life. It is a specialized amnesia service that creates a recording of the one and only memory that each person selects to keep for eternity. All other memories will be wiped away. What a choice that would be!*

*We have a much better choice to make: to recall as many memories as we can, and to interpret their truth as they formed and shaped us. Barbara King-solver wrote, "It's surprising how much of memory is built around things unnoticed at the time."[1] Let us see what we have noticed, and what formerly unnoticed or forgotten memory may escape the amnesia zone and become ours to own for eternity.*

*In the work here, we choose to remember. We choose self-awareness. We go back to the narratives that we do remember, we ask ourselves to look for new ones, and we start to view them all in ways that provide new options. We give our memories our best attention through the remembrance process, begin-ning with recalling.*

ONCE YOU BEGIN to "re-truth your past" with balanced and thorough reflection, you are more free to choose a future that you want, not the ones determined by past compressions.

Society and its institutions, and your specific interactions with them in the form of taunting fraternity brothers, an aunt who taught you how to garden, a lifelong friend who has always gotten who you are, a boss who demoted you over a mishandled project—all these and way more evoked and compressed you into the current version of you. Let's more thoroughly check out that interaction with those surroundings with a specific methodology. We want to fully understand our essential gifts on the plus side, and we want to redo our less-than-useful ways of being and doing on the minus side.

## Two Leaders Who Get It

Here are two examples of people who "truthed out" their yesterdays to good end. They chose not to forget, and they recalled.

### Example 1

Gifford Pinchot is a leader and an entrepreneur who first popped on the scene as the creator of intrapreneuring, a word he coined to describe the innovation process inside big companies.[2] If his name is at all familiar to you, your sense of history may tell you that an earlier Gifford Pinchot was the former governor of Pennsylvania and the first head of the U.S. Forest Service. The modern-day Gifford carries the family mantle of a world-class environmental leader. His cofounding of the Bainbridge Graduate Institute, the first to award an MBA for sustainable business, constitutes his latest signature creation.

Listen to him as he talks about a situation he encountered as a 10-year-old that had both good and not-so-good consequences for him.

66 When I was probably about 10, we moved from downtown New Haven to a suburb where we had a small farm. And that changed my life in two ways. I mean, one was of course all the glory of being in the outdoors—if I got mad at my parents, I could run into the woods until I got completely lost. And the joy of finding my way back home again would consume my whole attention, and I would be fine. I spent a lot of time alone in the woods and the various scrublands. And that was wonderful, but it also meant that all the after-school activities that other kids were engaged in, you know, the parties and so forth, were lost to me because I got a ride with one of the teachers who lived out where we were and at the end of the school day left and went home. So I missed out on a lot of the socialization that takes place in middle school, and I think that also had a lasting impact. I probably lack some skills that I would have otherwise had, and I also gained a whole bunch of skills in terms of finding my way around in nature. I became a very good shot with a slingshot, both the rubber band kind and the twirling-around-your-head kind.[3] 99

He neither romanticizes nor demonizes his past. He names it for what it was. The alone time had some downsides and some beautiful elements in the images he recalls.

### Example 2

You don't have to interview Valerie Morris for long to realize how skillfully she has harvested her past. The former CNN news anchor, for 15 years known as a world-class interviewer, is now a financial literacy advocate of major proportions in her current, encore career. She describes an evoking process from her youth:

66 As a girl, I was very used to adults, and I was very used to being lovingly included, and it didn't require a lot of discipline because it was just intuitive that one acts a certain way, that you're polite, that you're courteous, . . . and that you listen. I think one of the greatest gifts that my parents gave me by their example was the ability to listen. I think that that has made me an exceptionally good reporter. It has made me very capable of really sharing what people are saying rather than just waiting for them to finish so I can ask my next question. So that was a huge part of my past that played into my current work. If you really listen to people during an interview, I think that oftentimes things are revealed that you wouldn't have necessarily been privy to if you hadn't listened to the nuances in the conversation. I got it from my earliest years as a kid in this family that listened to everyone's story.[4] 99

Valerie's superstar status as a TV personality is rooted in her yesterdays and a strong awareness of what they taught her then and how they are still guiding her now. She attended to her story. Now you start carefully attending to yours.

## The Recall Process: An illustration

The goal of recalling is to bring the images and stories that define us to the surface of our mind. Recalling works with both our well-known memories and with those newly emerging.

The three steps to recalling, which is the first phase of remembrance, are as follows:

1. Identify the institution/social dynamic.
2. Recall the positive images or evocations.

3. Recall the negative images or compressions.

(For clarity's sake, a word about terms: I employ the terms *images* and *stories* almost interchangeably. A story is a series of images in motion. You can think of these terms in two reversible ways—for example, ice is frozen water; water is melted ice. An image contains a compressed story; a story is an image that moves into more images.)

### How I Victimized Myself through Comparison

Here is the illustration. As a young professional, I had unknowingly put limits on myself. As with most of us, my mental-emotional operating system had settled on a hidden self-limiting thought, acquired for no good reason, that prevented me from seeing who I was and what I could do.

Let me take you back so you can see how the three steps of recalling worked in a major growth decision I engineered that has helped me for 30 years.

### Step 1: Name the Institution/Social Structure

Peer groups, three of them—a very strong, lifelong high school peer group; and two less-intense professional/athletic peer groups in my early career in Washington, D.C.

### Group 1

From age 16 to 21, I find myself in a high-performing group of male peers that I come to love and respect throughout late high school and college. One of the guys in this group is the exceptionally talented writer David Quammen, quoted at the start of this chapter. He goes on to become the award-winning author of the stunning *Song of the Dodo: Island Biogeography in an Age of Extinction* (Simon & Schuster, 1996) and other superbly crafted books and articles in major magazines.

## Groups 2 and 3

Flash forward to my 26th year. I am in Washington, D.C., and I am working with bright emerging professionals, a few of whom publish as freelance writers. They talk about it casually, including the *TV Guide* cover article one of them got published. And also important, I play pick-up basketball with a number of guys in D.C. at a fairly high level.

### Steps 2 and 3: What Was Evoked and Compressed, and the Symbolic Images That Accompany Them

#### The Compression—from Group 1

David ("Q," as his friends call him) was, in my mind, *the* writer of the group. I knew that I could not write at his level. So I managed to exaggerate the gap between us, victimizing myself in a real way, and negated my ability to write books and articles with a beauty and utility of their own. This was a compression of my own making—Q did not foster it—which is where they all reside eventually, in our interpretations.

#### An Image from Group 1

I remember being at Yale with Q as a junior and feeling out of place around a few of his typically smart East Coast friends—I am an Irish-German kid from Iowa farmland. What am I doing in New Haven?

#### The Evocations—from Groups 2 and 3

Exposure to Group 2's casual and natural ownership of writing know-how ignited in me the thought that I could not entertain earlier, as long as I negatively compared myself with Q. I had my first positive writing thought—*I should try freelancing like these guys.*

With Group 3, I resumed an athletic passion from my past, playing pick-up basketball on the courts at the apartment complexes of D.C.'s suburbs. At its best, basketball here is played at a high level, and even at its worst, it is an example of young men of all backgrounds, from every corner of the world, cooperating and competing at a game they love.

### An Image from Group 2

Laughing at lunchtime in the cafeteria and seeing the *TV Guide* magazine with the author sitting next to me, conversing over a burger. I do *not* put these writers on a pedestal.

### An Image from Group 3

When we are being chosen for sides, the guy who is picking says, "Give me Rick Barry there," pointing to me, as Rick Barry was an NBA scoring star right then and I have a good jump shot.

### The Rest of the Story: I Get Published

I decide to write an article about playing basketball, and I get it published. Writers regularly tell stories about how they got their first article published. These are accounts of overcoming the sense of defeat caused by the backbreaking, heartbreaking effort of persisting through the heap of rejections and terse indifference of editors with too much to review and too many first-time authors trying to get published. (Even though blogging and self-publishing have multiplied the ways to publish, every writer still wants an article in *Rolling Stone* or *Harper's*, or a blog that has 100,000 visitors a day.) This is my very first attempt.

After a week of writing about basketball, I submit the piece. Two weeks later, without hearing from the editor, I call him (this is way pre-Internet), late on a Thursday. He is instantly apologetic and tells me the check is in the mail. My article appeared in that day's edition of the *Washington Post*.

I mumble a few words and we end the short conversation.

Here is an excerpt from the May 6, 1976 article:

## Four-on-Four: The Sandlot Subculture of the Basketball Junkie
*by John Schuster*

When the business and government offices in and around Washington close at the end of the day, young men from Beltsville to Occoquan gird mentally for the coming evening. Blank faces on the sub-35 males in the Shirley Express bus may conceal vivid fantasies of reverse lay-ups, floating jump shots, and behind-the-back dribbles. . . .

Inner D.C., like all large inner cities, has its own b-ball world, the breeding ground for tomorrow's college and pro stars. But nothing I have ever seen can compare to the white-collar suburban D.C. b-ball subculture. It is unique to Washington's concentration of young professional males, whose grade-school, high school, and even college athletic careers have passed some time ago, and who develop a camaraderie with each other by sharing the same passion for hard-played sandlot, playground, apartment-complex basketball. . . .

All of the rules and rituals of the sandlot subculture are based on the most fundamental of all the order-keeping systems—the "call-your-own" foul technique, truly an inviolate system. The player who thinks he is fouled calls it aloud, and his team gets the ball for a new offensive chance. The finer points of refereeing are surely lost in this system (offensive calls are not very common), but with a minimum amount of disagreement, bitching, and under-the-breath complaints—"I barely touched him"—the system works and the fouled player's word is taken.

Many stars of Washington's suburban sandlots will be leaving this highly transient area within a few years after their arrival. Their young careers will take them elsewhere, if not geographically, then socially and financially. Homes will be bought, children will grow up, and the leisure time for sandlot basketball will dwindle. The legs will lose their spring, and once-easy moves will become impossible. Growing old gracefully can mean leaving basketball for golf. The sandlot days will become memories.

But that's not yet. For now there are eight good outdoor months and four indoor when it's twice a week on the court. You work on your game, you daydream about your good shots, and you can't turn down the call: "Hey, you wanna play some four-on-four?"

This article is a lasting reminder of a little labor of love that could have stayed locked inside of me were it not for my becoming friendly with freelancers. The *Washington Post* on my first try—how cool was that!

Getting published in the *Post* was the beginning of my escape from the limiting, oh-so-reasonable falsehoods I had believed about my identity as a non-writer, non-artist, and non-businessman. I stumbled upon a process that I would later use regularly and that became the foundation for recalling and recasting. . . . I revisited my past to recast my stories about myself in the present. It started to dawn on me, as I was overcoming my amnesia, *though it was 10 years later that I fully got it*, that this was the way I could redirect my life and work. The good news is that we don't have to wait 10 years for these insights.

**Once we get how recall and the other steps of remembrance work, we can learn how to more quickly recognize what our experience is teaching us, which will enrich our thinking and ways of being.**

## Now It's Your Turn

My writing example is typical of what I find everywhere in people's thought patterns, even those of accomplished leaders. Huge falsehoods sneak in on occasion, such as, "People are impossible to work with" or "I have zero talent as a manager." But much more common are the small to medium misinterpretations of the past, such as, "I can't possibly work with a boss like this," or "I am always the smartest person in the room," or "I have to work 24/7 to get where I want to go."

---

These and about three million other, similar falsehoods infect our operating-system thoughts and our life and work capabilities. They look like true assessments but are really disguised thought bacteria that emerge from false comparisons, wrong conclusions, and mistaken logic.

---

Knowing the origins of our thought patterns can cut both ways. When we use origins to construct shallow rationalizations, or worse, to cement ourselves in our past, they aid stagnation. Our emphasis is in the opposite direction: to use origins for self-renewal.

The reason we go back to origins is that the memories that gave birth to a way of acting or thinking are where much of the power of our past lies. Origins are important for several reasons:

▶ When we feel the "truth" of the origin, knowing that the facts are always open to further interpretation, we can also see that a negative trait or belief is learned or acquired. If we learned it, we can unlearn it, at least to a significant degree.

*"I learned to be impatient with myself, and I can unlearn it for the benefit of myself, my team, and my family."*

► With the positive original memories, as time moves on, we can make wiser interpretations of the events than what the younger version of us could muster. *"I can really get that the big reason I so enjoy developing my team is that so many of my bosses helped me in big and little ways. What stories I have!"*

► With the negative ones, we can generate compassion for ourselves and others. This allows for a spaciousness within which we can overcome the bad habits that came with the negatives. *"I can see now, finally, that those endless conflicts with my boss were more about my high standards than about my ego."*

► Finally, origin stories, deliberately brought to mind and pondered, provide needed nuances of self-knowledge. Without refined distinctions, we cannot deploy our best selves into the wide array of settings we encounter.

"I am an extravert" is one level of self-knowledge. *"I am an extravert with Italian roots from New York City. I have a tendency to fill in gaps in others' thinking and to never be satisfied with the first attempt at anything"* is another level.

Not all of your powerful memories are origins, of course. Other important ones add momentum to traits already in existence. Still others, like my *Washington Post* memory, are more of a turnaround from a negative to a positive.

## RECALL EXERCISE: EVOKED, COMPRESSED, RELEASED

The exercise that follows takes you through a review of how you fared in getting to this point in your work and life. You already know at least some, if not a lot, about this. But you have most likely not looked at the how-did-I-get-here question in the way it is presented. This exercise, and the next two, guides you to do the reflection that erodes the amnesia and leads to insight and action. Do the work in the exercises, and you will address the core work of this book.

So now we muster some courage, stirring up both the joy and anxiety that come when we recall our encounter with non-paradise. It's like going on a roller-coaster or a long ski run. I was reminded of this recently when taking my grandkids to Disney World.

This first step of recall catalogues your memories and images. Steps 2 and 3 take you more to the interpretation and impact of those memories. First we make the list and retrieve, and then we take a comprehensive look at how you and non-paradise got along.

---

**Consider this a kind of self-awareness archaeology, a digging expedition of remembrance and truth seeking.**

---

Doing this thinking systematically is the key to garnering more of the truth. If you are right-brained and metaphoric, and can't remember the last time you were systematic about anything, don't worry. This exercise provides the structure for you and still depends on your recall of narrative examples. Left-brained analytical types, enjoy this chapter: it can be quite quantitative as you track what parts of the story come primarily from your education, your region, or a key family relocation when you were 12.

This first exercise, like the next two steps of remembrance, is for people who are in the normal range of recall with ample memories. If you can't retrieve many of your memories, keep in mind that people have widely varying degrees of recall; record the memories you can, and use the exercise at the end of the chapter on recalling with others.[5]

### Guidelines

Here again are the three steps of recall:

1. Identify the institution/social dynamic.
2. Recall the positive images or evocations.
3. Recall the negative images or compressions.

There are two primary methods for completing the exercise, explained below. Use the one you like, or combine them if you want, or use them both in the sequence you like (and feel free to make up your own versions, of course).

### Method 1: The Circle with Pluses and Minuses

Use the "Impact on Self" diagram below to list the evocations and compressions that you recall. The way I do this in workshops is with little pluses and minuses, as shown in the diagram, one circle per institution. The second circle has an education example for you.

You will need several circles, one for each institution, as you explore the different institutions/social structures, so make as many circles as you need (or go to my website, www.johnpschuster.com/thepowerofyourpast).

This is the part that makes it systematic. Most of us have family memories as well as memories from some of the institutions. But we have forgotten or minimized important ones that, once uncovered and explored, create the platform for growth.

The circles that include many more pluses than minuses stand for the "good" social structures, of course, the ones that evoked and created capacity. These are the places to visit as you want to reclaim new gems or polish them anew. The reverse is true for the damage control/repair you have

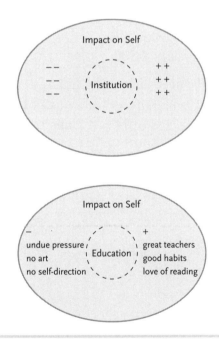

**IMPACT ON SELF TEMPLATE**

had to do in the minus-dominant circles. They point to the recasting, reinterpreting work ahead.

Some of the images you list on either the plus or the minus side may have lasted for years in your memory, and others, long forgotten, may come up fresh. That is how this works.

### Method 2: A More Linear Approach

We will use the table on the following page for this exercise. (It is available for download on my website, www.johnp schuster.com/thepowerofyourpast.)

You will see the three steps in the columns across the top; these are your prompts to explore your yesterdays. A quick scan of the columns shows that column two asks for pluses, the evocations and their images; and column three asks for minuses, the compressions and their images. We will work on the meaning of these evocations and compressions in the next steps.

On the vertical axis down the left side you see the institutions and social structures of non-paradise that you encountered. They are in no particular order, since only you know which of the institutions or social structures were significant for you, and which ones you have explored the most.

The institutions/social structures of greatest importance for most of us are parents, of course, and enough has been written about that, for good reason, to fill a few libraries. As one of my mentors used to say, "You never get over your parents—if they were the world's best or the most rotten, or whatever, you have them forever." So fill out a few columns on them if you want, and watch out for getting stuck in parent stories with sentimentalizing or demonizing. I was a second child, and as sibling order sometimes can predict,

## The Recall Process

| Institution encountered and experienced | What it evoked: *The images* | What it compressed: *The images* |
| --- | --- | --- |
| School/education | | |
| Parents | | |
| Region | | |
| Moves that affected me | | |
| Extended family | | |
| Religion | | |
| Gender | | |
| Country/nation | | |
| Race/ethnicity | | |
| Health factors | | |
| Other categories you want to use | | |
| Glee club | | |
| First software job at company | | |

I found that peer groups were more important than parents in many ways.

On the left are the major social structures, such as family, gender, race, religion, and ethnicity. As you spend time contemplating them with this methodology, expect to stir up new memories and images. There are also some less common ones, like "region" and "health factors," that can be just as powerful as the others, depending on your life. And be sure to add your own specifics with the factors/institutions that deserve their own category.

These less common social dynamics are usually very important. I can't overemphasize that. One category for me would be "cousins," and another "aunts"—both had a significant impact on me as I look at the evocation/plus side. Another would be "region": my Iowa roots are filled with pluses and minuses. (The opening line from the hero of *Prince of Tides*, Tom Wingo, is "My wound is geography. It is also my anchorage, my port of call."[6])

Be creative and true to your life as you remember it. Concentrate on the social structures, general or specific, and the periods that you want to examine. The ones listed here are quite enough to get you going and to explore in the weeks ahead.

## How Much Time Should I Invest?

In the many workshops where I have facilitated this exercise, I have frequently had the comment, "Wow, this is rich—I need more time to think on this." You might ask, "How long do I spend on this exercise—a day, a week, a month?" Yes, all of the above. It can be useful to come back to the exercise often for some weeks ahead, to keep embellishing your recall. Eventually, you will come back to it occasionally, as needed or as new images occur to you. The task of harvesting your past through remembrance goes on throughout your life.

## A Few Options

One option is to start with one era in your life, such as high school, and recall all of the social dynamics in that time (friends, family, school, religion, sports, debate, the region).

Another option is take one institution at a time, such as education, and follow it through your life. Then expand from there to other institutions. Over the next few weeks, I encourage you to take several hours of solo time to recall your past through the lenses of the institutions and social structures as you encountered them. Honestly assess what was evoked and what was shriveled by your brief or lengthy, glorious or dastardly, encounter with non-paradise. Three hours is a good start. You can do more with loved ones and friends and your coach later—more on that at the end of the chapter.

---

When you reflect on your past with a high intention, you are embarking on a journey of sacred commemoration, a noble remembering of your life—the triumphant and healthy, the damaging and unhealthy, the normal and undramatic. This is your history, your high story, waiting to be tapped.

## Final Instructions: Muster Up Some Inner Strength

Central to this book, and one of the chief ingredients for revealing the unknown magic of your yesterdays, is courage. It takes courage to peer into your internal mental/emotional dynamics, the ones that comprise your beliefs and hidden thought patterns, and to investigate what is true and useful and what is untrue and falsely limiting. It takes courage to see things as they are and were, to see what is and was, and to name it. It takes strength to review your life, allowing a more authentic version of you to emerge so that you can pour yourself into work worthy of you.

I have included the example on the next several pages to show you how the process looks after you have started the work. I use my life to some extent here, and others' as well. So gird your loins, memory stalker. Get ready for the trip.

## FAQs That Emerge When Doing This Exercise, with Answers

*Should I spend more time on the minuses?* Sure, if you haven't addressed them. And trace the unsatisfactory events of the present—regular anxiety over an exacting boss, procrastination on big projects—to early similar events, so that you see the thread. The thread is everything. Anxiety today is "the psyche's signal system, alerting us to what needs an updating."[7]

*What if I can't remember much?* Go find some friends or colleagues you had at that time or in that school or those work periods. Ask your parents and siblings what they recall. You can usually get all kinds of images and

## IMPACT ON SELF TABLE

| INSTITUTION ENCOUNTERED AND EXPERIENCED | WHAT IT EVOKED: *THE IMAGES* | WHAT IT COMPRESSED: *THE IMAGES* |
|---|---|---|
| School/education | Love of learning study habits, sports, ability to think critically. | Study till I drop, overstudying and cramming, not thinking creatively. |
| | *IMAGES* First place in the comprehensive exam; seeing the list with my name on top. | *IMAGES* Reading two novels, *Dr. Zhivago* and *Emma*, in one week; pushing for A's while not learning; absence of the arts. |
| | Father Savage lecture on *1984* by Orwell and Big Brother. | |
| Parents (a whole chapter is possible here for most) | Humor, love, fun and silliness, love of learning, sports, reading, sense of fairness, hard work, reverence for life. | Artistic pursuits, ability to feel/ express anger, questioning authority, working with my hands. |
| | So much to be grateful for. | So much to regain. |
| | *IMAGES* Fishing with Dad, laughing with family, church, trips in the car across the Midwest. | *IMAGES* Shamed by spilling, not engaging conflict (no images because they were absent). |

| Institution encountered and experienced | What it evoked: *The images* | What it compressed: *The images* |
| --- | --- | --- |
| Aunts | Freedom, compe-tence, belonging in the world.<br><br>*IMAGES*<br>Sitting on a blanket under the stars with Aunt Alice, the teacher.<br><br>Laughing in the kitchen with Helen and Dorothy. Aunt Anne's pies in her little kitchen. | None I can think of. |
| Region | | |
| Moves that affected me | | |
| Extended family | | |
| Religion | | |
| Gender | | |
| Country/nation | | |

(continued)

## IMPACT ON SELF TABLE

| INSTITUTION ENCOUNTERED AND EXPERIENCED | WHAT IT EVOKED: *THE IMAGES* | WHAT IT COMPRESSED: *THE IMAGES* |
|---|---|---|
| Race/ethnicity | | |
| Health | | |
| Other factors | | |

stories. Look through your photo albums. Look through yearbooks and old work products from early jobs you saved. Go through the boxes in your basement that evoke memories. Look around your house for tokens and objects that carry memories.

*What other questions can I use?* Hundreds, I imagine. Here are a few more (with prompts), and you can make up your own:

▶ Who were my best teachers, and what did I learn? Worst damage incurred?

▶ What are some favorite sayings of my parents? (Life is a box of chocolates, or a battle, or a quest.)

▶ What did my region teach me? (Midwest—patience and the seasons; California—endless play.)

*Why are the images important?* The collected images from our past are not merely the brain's super DVD for recording memories. By images, we mean the pictures and sounds, the smells and feelings—all the sensory inputs that stay in our memories. Images are more important than recordings. They contain compressed data laced with meaning. They are worth a thousand words because they carry the mental-emotional codifications for what you are good at, what you can give yourself wholeheartedly to, what energizes you.

*What if what I remember is different from what others remember?* This is less about accuracy and more about the impressions and interpretations you have made of your yesterdays. Be open to others' versions, accept their value, and let go of your own version when you are ready. That is how you experienced the event and represented it to yourself. If you want to change the representation, it is best to start with the current one you have and not one borrowed from others.

*What if I remember a whole bunch of new stuff?* Good—that is one of the reasons to do it.

*What if I get compulsive and start to recall the stories again and again?* Go read the funnies and talk a walk with your dog. Lighten up. Stories and images are meant for you to use, not to obsess over in an endless loop replay. You are resurrecting these for the present and future you, remember.

*What if I get sad or angry?* Good—that is telling you something. Let it be, and don't get stuck in it. Emotions are meant to flow through you. Read the "warning" in the introduction again. If the sadness or anger is big, go find a counselor or therapist. Don't make decisions based on the feelings, and don't bury them. The burying is what is blocking you.

## ▶ SUMMARY

Our destiny takes shape when the person we were born to be intersects with the happenstances of our life. As we grow into adulthood, our potential clashes and blends with the realities of the social structures in non-paradise. As an adult, then, if our job is to live our destiny fully, we must go back to the roots of our calling, the stories that formed us. Our quest to put our native talents and gifts to work will never result in a perfect deployment, but it can be forged into a close approximation. We need to rediscover the gifts handed to us and undo the compressions we endured.

The lyrics to "The Scientist," by superband Coldplay, put it well:

> *Nobody said it was easy,*
> *No one ever said it would be so hard,*
> *I'm going back to the start.*

The recall exercise in this chapter begins to reveal and redirect our operating-system-level thoughts. We do this through images—they are at the core of our ability to see, feel, and sense beyond the literal and into the thoughts and forms behind the surface thoughts.

As you face the questions of today—career, work, relationships—you are better equipped to find the inspiration and imagination you need for a choice about the future—"Does taking my career this direction make sense?"—if you can source the imagination and inspiration (all those pluses) from your past. You also stare down the fear of a tough choice ahead—"Am I ready for this promotion?"—when you know the sources of your fears and constrictions (all the minuses) and prevent them from limiting your thinking and your possibilities.

Let's continue the work into the next chapter.

▷ *Core takeaway idea:* When we recall our memories with curiosity, we can think in new ways about them, and can begin to dismantle our habituated views of who we are and aren't, resetting the specifications of our lives.

### ▶ STATEMENTS OF INTENT TO ENGAGE THE WILL AND FIRE THE IMAGINATION

I revisit my past with courage, seizing the truth about the person I am as I creatively will myself to do my best work.

I reclaim the power of my yesterdays by giving them attention and probing for the deep layers of meaning they store.

By taking the time to recall my life, I refresh my goals and reset the arc of my life's path.

### ▶ ADDITIONAL OPTIONAL EXERCISE: USING DIALOGUE WITH OTHERS TO INCREASE RECALL

One way to increase recall and the images from your past is to talk to friends and family members who have memories of the event. In talking to my sisters on trips and holidays, I have gotten great insight into our lives on the joys of our family, the many moves we endured and then benefited from, and even on the role of alcohol. At reunions, I have had conversations that have also expanded my recall.

Invite three members of the family to join you in conversations, and tell them what you are up to. Then return to the exercise and see what you come up with.

*As a mature leader, you . . . invent who you are.*
*You are responsible for who you are, regardless of your*
*origins—your parents, your education, your ethnicity.*
*You freely accept your origins, or reject them, or modify*
*them, or supersede them.*

—PETER KOESTENBAUM, *KOESTENBAUM'S*
*WEEKLY LEADERSHIP THOUGHT*

# Chapter Four: Reclaim

*In* The Bourne Identity, *the hero, Jason Bourne, suffers total amnesia. He agonizes over his high functioning with very select and advanced skills without knowing how or why he acquired them: "I can tell you the license plate numbers of all six cars outside. I can tell you that our waitress is left-handed and the guy sitting up at the counter weighs 215 pounds and knows how to handle himself. I know the best place to look for a gun is the cab of the gray truck outside. . . . Now why would I know that? How can I know that and not know who I am?"*

*Through and around the car chases and high-adventure sequences is a forlorn hero asking the big questions of identity and redemption—"Who am I? What did I do? Can I escape what I am and be something different and more?"*

*As we reinvent and express ourselves, we all ask ourselves similar questions.*

WE FINISHED THE recall exercise in the previous chapter. It is time to experience the next step in edging us toward the truth of our potential, our values, our essence. Of the three opportunities we have been address-ing—identity, potential, and self-direction—this chapter mostly focuses on identity. Here we continue to gain deeper insight by moving toward some forgotten, not allowed, or underappreciated truths.

In the last chapter, we recalled—excavated our current truths through images. We recalled the whole enchilada, everything significant we could, without regard for its impact on us. In this chapter, we reclaim—analyze and amplify the positive truths anew. Here, we select and deal only with the positives, the evocations. In the next chap-ter, we recast—analyze only the negatives and replace our interpretations with more fitting truths.

We continue this direction for one reason: to increase your self-knowledge.

**Without intimate knowledge, a deep and nuanced appre-ciation of our core selves, we cannot create our life's core work. We go after as much of the truth as we can find. We grow to the degree that we can stand the truth.**

The truth of who you are; the questions around which you formulate a life; where and how you accrued the best of your identity, the worst, and everything in between—all this vital information is cast in the images you carry around. Your history is a series of images and stories.

## Two More Leaders Who Get It

Here are two more examples of people who "truthed out" their yesterdays to good end. They reclaimed.

*Example 1*

David Dotlich, author of bestsellers on leadership,[1] recounts how, when he was 25, getting kicked out of a country and the lifelong images of trans-African travel filled with strangers in conflict were the beginning of his life quest.

> You know, I actually went to South Africa to study in a graduate program. I was doing research in a township during apartheid, and they asked me to leave the country fairly quickly. My visa wasn't renewed. And so with a colleague I decided to drive from South Africa to London through Africa. So we did that. We bought a couple of Land Rovers and we advertised for people, and got 15 people to come with us. This guy that I knew had actually done this before. So we had 15 people from nine different countries traveling together for four months in two Land Rovers, camping out at night, driving through the jungle and the Sahara Desert and everything. And you know when you think about that, the hardship of traveling in Africa was hard. But the really hard part was that the 15 people did not like or get along well with each other . . . a lot of conflict. There were a lot of cross-cultural issues, the personalities didn't jell, and four months is a long time when people don't like each other. . . . When I got back, I got really interested in groups. How did groups behave, why don't some groups jell, why do people under stress behave so badly? It sent me on a . . . lifelong interest in human relations and group psychology and group work. The point is, at 25 I didn't know what I wanted to do, and this experience for me was kind of pivotal in thinking about what I wanted to do.[2]

David attends to the roots of his lifelong quest, one he is still pursuing now, as a seasoned professional at the height of his influence.

## *Example 2*

Barbara Roberts whirrs, hums, and bubbles through life. She is a whirlwind of energy and networks whose career on Wall Street, and dedication to helping entrepreneurs of all stripes and businesswomen in general find some of the success she had in her career, provide her with an original, multi-angled view of the world. She reclaims her past in all kinds of ways—here is one of them.

❝ I guess my big purpose . . . is helping women particularly get their fair share of the political and economic pie. . . . In my early days on Wall Street, I have to honestly say I was there just to cause trouble about raising awareness about the nonsense and the craziness of how women were being treated in the work environment. . . . But the two big lawsuits—class action suits in the mid '70s against Chase and Merrill—were actually the beginning of making relatively regular women kind of believe that you actually had the right and the responsibility and also the possibility of going far in business. But I absolutely remember in my first years working in Wall Street that I had very little expectation of being able to get anywhere. That still was the mood of the time. . . .

I was the first woman on the board of directors of Dean Witter. The way I got there is in 1984 I think the Dow was 750, which is kind of amazing. I actually wrote a paper on demographic changes that would take the market to 5000 by the year 2000. Of course, it ended being closer to 12,000 by that year, but [this paper] earned me a place on the board of directors.

The women's thing has a long history. In actual fact, I led a strike in second grade because girls were not allowed to carry the American flag. Now where this came from in second grade—I had two very strong grandmothers . . . the only thing I can point to is that this started and in only the second grade.

We won! We went on strike for like 20 minutes. We went out to the playground and weren't coming back.[3] 🙶🙷

Grandmothers and a successful work stoppage in second grade are the kinds of images reclaimed anew in each retelling, channeling Barbara's energy for the work of a lifelong change agent/provocateur. In the images of David and Barbara, you can hear both their will and imagination, the core of reclaiming.

## Reclaiming by Thinking Past the Facts

The point of systematically reviewing your yesterdays is not to craft an overanalyzed person fitting into an overcalculated life. We ferret out everything important that we can, our thoughts that influence us the most, not because our memories have all the facts, but because they tell us what is important in our thoughts behind our thoughts.

And there is a catch.

If we think about our past from the factual level only, we are like a Cyclops with one eye—we see just the facts and only the facts, and miss the depth of perception that comes with being bi-ocular. With one-eyed, facts-only thinking, the images pile up, warehoused and lifeless, confining our history to a collection of events with no compelling or unifying thread. This is not much better than the forgetfulness of ignoring and amnesia.

---

If we raise our thinking, however, and go at our past from multiple levels and with both eyes, our recalled yesterdays are a living 3-D movie for the emerging truth of who we are, what we are becoming, and where our commitments can take us.

---

Instead of sitting in our memories taking up space, these same images, the ones that carry the facts, stir our imaginations and amplify our choices. As I grew into more understanding of my work through my yesterdays, I came to realize that my past may be irrevocable and fixed, but my understanding and interpretation of it is not. I can cast my imagination and mature understanding into my yesterdays to live and work anew. This is what Barbara Roberts and David Dotlich are doing.

Some people function without a useful or usable story within which to place their storehouse of images. They tote around a collage of separate images that provide no useful flow through time or into meaning. We have all watched young people with a ton of talent struggle for life cohesion as they experience the confusing array of life events. And I have coached executives in their 50s with genuine business genius who have never pieced together a career worthy of their talents. Instead, they settle for the mainstream of the cultural story, the "I am a senior vice president of overhead and I make good money" story. They wonder why they feel less than fulfilled.

## USING OUR RECORDED IMAGES TO SHAPE OUR DESTINY

People have different levels of capability to utilize images well and to think imaginatively about their yesterdays. This is no surprise, given our blind spot about our yesterdays' ability to contribute to our tomorrows. The following construct describes the level of thinking effectiveness required to take the images in your life from recorded memories to a destiny story. It should look familiar— the same levels were highlighted in chapter 2.

Here is an illustration of how the same images, viewed factually or imaginatively, create different interpretations of our experience.

*Level 1:* The basic images are here and not much else. It is surface thinking that has a random quality, creating a series of jobs but no inner advancement.

> Example: *I went to school in California and learned art there from an engaging teacher. This is when I first learned about art.*

*Transition from Level 1 to Level 2:* Eventually for most, we start to turn the collection of events into a story with themes, creating the glimpses of meaning that source a career.

> Example: *I was born in sunny San Jose and I went to the public schools, and in sixth grade my ex-hippie art teacher turned me on to creativity in the studio. I still remember the day I felt I could be good at art. It was the beginning of my career.*

*Level 2:* Well-defined individuals have collected and examined the images from their past, the ones with the operating-system thought-behind-the-thought power, and have harvested their unique history. They have woven the images into a narrative with subplots and themes pointing to universal truths.

> Example: *I was born to be an artist. My story begins, really, with an art teacher who believed in me. She wore these outrageous pink outfits, was totally absorbed in the quest for beauty, and evoked out of me the gifts that were dormant, and may have stayed dormant, were it not for her laughter, her passion for beauty, her attention to me. This is when I began my quest to express beauty.*

Like a novelist who knows her art, we can take our unique history to the high level of meaning, also referred to as myth, saga, destiny, or path. Myth is the level of story that contains the lasting principles, where, like Luke Sky-walker, we invoke "the Force," and we live out our largest story. If you are faith based, this is you talking it over with God. (In Jewish Seder practices, the participants recall in the first person, participating in the memory and its con-

---

### Early Training on Fiscal Responsibility

M. K. Larson is the executive director and steward of a foundation that her grandfather started. As executive director of the M. R. and Evelyn Hudson Foundation, she does the important work of seeding nonprofits in education and the arts.

Listen to this image, a very short conversation, about her checkbook in hand.

> I was sitting at my desk (as a teenager) looking at my bills, and my grandfather asked me what I was doing. "Well, I'm paying a bill." He came over, picked it up, and looked at it, and his face got really red. He went like, "UGGGH!" and got very upset at me as I was getting ready to pay a bill with a finance charge. He was very angry about that, and he said, "I'll tell you what I'll do. This one time I'll pay it, but if I ever see a finance charge again, I'll take it away from you forever." And just that one day, that one moment in my past, helped save thousands and thousands of dollars throughout my life because it was a fundamental lesson about tools and about money that I didn't know.[4]

Today she and her team in Dallas/Ft. Worth give out millions in grants yearly.

She knows that this conversation with her grandpa will continue to inform the truth of her life and work. This is going past the simple facts, and working with the checkbook image at the identity level. She reclaims her stewardship every time she recalls the story.

tinuing meaning in present-day life. Here, memory participates powerfully in the present.)

This destiny-level thinking is what we need to craft our lifework. This is where we discover our possibilities. Here the images inform an identity, and a destiny story grasps its roots. Remembering at this level is *remembrance*, with elements of recalling, reclaiming, and recasting. It is a spiritual, soul-forming practice.

Here is the construct in table form.

This narrative-forming work, allowing the images of your yesterdays to indicate meaning and truth, is a core task in authoring your own life and work. There are different levels of writers, from people who can't write—because it is not their thing, for whatever reason—to authors who can write entertaining novels, to authors who can create lasting beauty and real literature. Movies are the same, from those that waste our time and money to those that stir our souls with lasting beauty.

We can't all write, but we all have images that we can recall and reclaim.

## SURFACE AND DESTINY THINKING ABOUT IMAGES

| OUR IMAGE-BASED THOUGHTS | HOW WE EXPERIENCE THEM | IMPLICATIONS FOR OUR WORK AND LIFE |
|---|---|---|
| **Level 1** Surface thoughts that come up on my mental screen. | Unconnected episodes or a story with no significance. | Series of jobs, or a goal like making money, accruing titles, and other dead ends. |
| Images without a plot to connect them. | A drama but not a quest, like bad TV. | Win a race not worth running. Can create advancement without purpose. |
| **Transition from Level 1 to Level 2** Images start to create a plot. | A story begins to take shape as the images become embedded with lessons. | We make wiser choices; direction and use of gifts begins. |
| **Level 2** Deeper operating-system thoughts determined by our compressions and evocations. Images form a saga, a story with human and heroic qualities. | Meaning becomes clear for longer periods, and both the barren and fruitful times create a rhythm of quest and next questions to address. | Self-expression and a unique contribution are felt regularly. |

Remembrance, and reclaiming in particular, distills the essentials. It is what creates the imaginative story you need for your work and life—the expansive story you can lean into, not the fact-restricted story of what has happened to you.

## How Yesterdays Inspire:
## Lent, Coors, and Redemption

Like M. K. Larson's checkbook, some of our images can turn into essential narratives. Some images contain more lessons than others and become candidates for stories laced with overarching meaning that guide us into our best work in the world. These higher levels won't happen without reclaiming and the imagination of Level 2 thinking.

Here is an example from my life that illustrates how images, recalled and reflected on, provide meaning and even inspiration that we can claim and reclaim as often as we need them.

*Note:* The following story is not in any way meant to glorify alcohol. My German-Irish family has endured plenty of heartache over alcohol's destructive potential.

66 My mom really liked beer. When she gave it up for Lent one year, it was a big deal, a sizable sacrifice. If you are raised Catholic, Lent is a big deal, as it is for most Christians. It is the 40 days before Easter, which prepare the faithful for the event that caps the whole story of incarnation.

Mom decided this particular year not to drink beer for 40 days and nights. The nights were the real challenge, as every evening, with Dad—or without, if he was traveling—she would open a

Coors (when we lived in Cheyenne) or a Hamm's (when we lived in the Twin Cities) or a Hudepohl (when Cincinnati became her long-lasting home). Drinking beer never meant that she couldn't function fully as a mom and wife. She had an attitude, and that signature laugh, that let her enjoy her life through those responsibilities, even with the many losses that came with growing old.

As Lent continued that year, the pressure built up for her. The internal pressure of a craving not acted upon is the spiritual idea, of course. She had chosen beer as the item to give up for all of Lent because she was drawn to it. The sacrifice feature of Lent is a part of the preparation. In "giving something up," the three words for the practice that our nun teachers encouraged us to use, we would give up an automatic creature comfort and replace it with a higher, more elevated thought. With self-sacrifice we could take our thoughts off automatic and do and be something more loving or more Christ-like, even if it was minor.

On the 40th morning after Fat Tuesday, we attend Easter Mass as a family: my very devout and scrupulous dad; my faithful, less devout mom; my younger sister not yet asking the religious questions that college brings; and a searching-for-meaning, late-adolescent version of me. We sing Handel's "Messiah" at St. Vivien's Church and celebrate the Resurrection and the Great Triumph. We drive home to our modest home in our modest car as a foursome, my older sister still in the last year of her five years in the convent.

My mom whisks into the kitchen to prepare the full-out Easter Sunday brunch. A few minutes later, changed into less churchy clothes, I scoot down the stairs and turn the corner from the hallway to the little kitchen—"the one-butt kitchen," as she called it—and I hear a familiar sound, a sound that had not been heard for 40 evenings.

You probably can guess it.

Pphhhhht!!

Mom pops off the tab on a beer. And then that big voice of hers rings out. "Ahhh—lleluia-a-a-a!" as if Handel were conducting the chorus from the top of the stove.

Life is back to normal. Lent, suffering, beer, and redemption come together in a moment of joyous release. 🙽

## IMAGES, MEANING, AND EMBEDDED DEPTH

This is a fun story by itself. But the lessons here are what we are after. The first lesson is that even a powerful and now-unforgettable story like this is indeed forgettable. I had amnesia about this whole episode for more than two decades, as it finally came to mind many years after it happened. The second lesson is how the image of my mom popping open the Easter beer can with the kitchen-reverberating "Alleluia!" makes up part of *my* mythology, my destiny. It is an image that, when I dwelled on it some, elevated itself to the level of a universal symbol. It has become a part of my psychological heritage, my identity. Through reclaiming, I own it as an essential story—my mom's life and her daily joy and sense of fun are both what I have been given in life and what I have to offer. If that is her major gift to the world, I also choose it as one I hope to incarnate and pass on.

I use that alleluia energy as an essential part of my work. I rely on this uplifting energy when I teach or coach—it fosters the uplifting possibilities always at play. Rita's unconquerable heart and sheer fun are what I want to be in my work. Alleluia it is. I sing onstage now, after having taken up the guitar in my mid-50s—something I had not done the first 30-plus years of my work life (itself a compression story worth telling, but not here)—because song and alleluia is in me.

I have loads of other images/symbols/stories like this, some evocations and some compressions:

My speaking mentor, Bill McGrane Sr., giving me monster hugs at age 26 and asserting "TUA," total unconditional acceptance, as a life mantra for self and others.
My dad doing his work at the dining room table at night.
My sister and I always getting straight A's in order to test our potential and to keep harmony at home.
My coach yelling across the gym, "You are a shooter," when I was a 5-foot-3 freshman with no confidence. (This story is central to my previous book, *Answering Your Call: A Guide to Living Your Deepest Purpose.*[5]) These images and a lot more make up my internal library of essential stories.

The point here is not my images. It is those of M. K. Larson, Tommy Emmanuel, Barbara Roberts. It is the images of all of us. We are all packed with such imagery, and we can see it if we pay attention and let some of our amnesia slip away. Many of the images don't rise to the level of truth or meaning, of course, nor should they. Even if an image is fascinating, like escaping an accident by luck, it may not qualify as a destiny story of remembrance. If it doesn't carry moral significance, identity-laden material, and the deep elements of a life, the image won't help you to define or re-possibilitize.

By way of preparation for your remembrance work at the end of this chapter, let me be more explicit about my understanding of the story of my mom's Easter beer. It exists at both levels of our interpretive thought.

▶ At Level 1: a simple image of a funny memory of my mom.

▶ As a transition to Level 2: my mom took her religion seriously enough to make a real sacrifice during Lent—another legitimate interpretation.

▶ Or, taken at Level 2, the image infuses my deepest story, my sense of who I am and what I am supposed to do with my time on the planet. I resonate with the joy, silliness, and depth of it all.

---

**By musing on our images from yesterday, we commemorate our lives and work. We give our soul the gift of its deep history. We muse on the higher forces that show up in the little things, the ones that formed us, that are still forming us and lead to our best work.**

---

## STRANGE LITTLE IMAGES, COMPELLING BIG MEANINGS

When I work with people as they reclaim their essential stories, they are sometimes confused by the smallness or strangeness of the images that they build their stories around. Isn't this can-of-beer image kind of a weird choice for a personal mythology? One of my clients was drawn to an image of herself in a tutu as a little girl—its innocence and artistic beginnings—and it surprised her. Shouldn't the compelling memory be the day you met Nelson Mandela at the United Nations? Or the minute you walked off campus with a degree after nine long years of night school?

Little images like a beer in the kitchen become essential in our lifework's story for three reasons.

First, we organize and represent our experience of life idiosyncratically. That is why we think like artists when we practice remembrance. The artist in us, and we all have one, is seized by the images of the compressions and evocations that form our truth. It is not the facts, but rather the images that capture the meaning behind the facts, that matter.

The beer story had so many key ingredients for me: Irish, Catholic, alcohol and the suffering in the family, rituals, Lent, sacrifice, dedication to higher levels of being, fun, music—so many primordial elements that came together.

These elements are bigger than me, and you, and our understanding of things at Level 1, so we must give them their due at Level 2 when we surrender to them and subordinate the facts to the meaning underneath the facts.

Second . . .

**You don't so much choose the images as much as the images choose you, with meaning marinated into them.**

They can seize you at the time they happen, of course, but many only seize you later, when your imaginative and wiser memory can grasp their significance in depth. You have to let yourself dwell on these seizures and let your mind and heart be confounded by the depth that an image with a loaded back story, like a beer on Easter, can carry.

Third . . .

Yes, meeting Mr. Mandela is also a candidate for remembrance and your personal mythology. In fact, you have hundreds, if not endless, candidates for the symbolic images that make up your high story and your work destiny. Some are big efforts and travails, and some are little one-offs— checkbooks, beers, a tutu—that inexplicably create a soul-quake.

"Give your life the dignity of your attention," says Tom Wingo in *Prince of Tides*.[6] Your best attention includes your imagination and Level 2 thinking. We can't control what images have the power. They just do. Recasting depends upon the healing power of these images. Healing is like the creative process; the images themselves do the work.

This is poetic imagination—how the artist in all of us three-dimensionally captures the essence of our experience. What we are about here is using our yesterdays to amplify the inherent dignity of our life and work, the daily soulfulness weakened by facts-only, one-eyed thinking and memories left unattended.

Here is how to do it.

## Reclaim Exercise: Distilling the Evocations

One more thought before you start:

You may think that since you can't verify the facts around your stories from memory, you ought not to build lessons around them. Do not let that be an impediment. *The reclaim exercise is not exclusively, or even primarily, about historical accuracy. It is about meaning and growth. It is about imaginative impact and power.*

Remembrance concerns your interpretation and representation of the facts. That is where the new possibilities reside. Author Thomas Moore writes, "Nicholas [of Cusa] noted that, rooted in holy uncertainty, we are left with approximations. . . . The point in thinking is to reach the far edge of understanding and to stand there in wonder."[7]

In the following reclaim exercise, you learn to live with ambiguity, stand in wonder at the images from your yesterdays, and allow those images to teach you what you need. There is a four-month ride out of Africa, a checkbook and a scolding from your grandpa, and a beer on Easter Sunday in the kitchen, waiting to gift you.

### Guidelines

Here are the three steps of reclaiming, shown in the chart below:

1. Identify and analyze the impacts of the evocations.
2. Reclaim their power by unfreezing and updating.
3. Apply the new lessons to current settings.

Note: For any newly recalled stories, use the same chart with a few modifications.

### Step 1: Identify and Analyze the Impact of the Evocation Stories and Images

The stories that came to mind in the last chapter are a place to start—school and family and early bosses and all the other institutions that evoked you (and, of course, any new images that occur to you). These already-known stories and images will likely hold previous explanations. They are not wrong, but they may need updating. The next step, unfreezing, allows new lessons to emerge. Use the table at the end of this chapter, also available on my website, at www.johnpschuster.com/thepowerofyourpast.

### Step 2: Reclaim Their Power by Unfreezing and Updating

We unfreeze the image for new insight when we ask questions like these:

> ▶ What is it about the image that pulls me in?
> ▶ Why *that* image—what in the back story of the image makes it so vital?
> ▶ What feelings emerge for me as I dwell on this image? What thoughts?
> ▶ What is the image trying to teach me? Where does my imagination take this?

This is the step we need to practice the most in order to harvest the power of our yesterdays. Use the examples provided to spark your own thinking, and surrender to the deeper meanings of the stories. We amplify when we imagine. This important step is the wisdom distillation that began with Step 1, recall.

### Step 3: Apply the Meaning Level to Your Current Situation

Once you have new meanings, look at how the issues in your current life can be addressed with the energy that emerges with these possibilities.

### ▶ SUMMARY

Our yesterdays are gone but not frozen. We recall and reclaim, and by doing so renew our sense of destiny and sculpt new work. This process of high remembering rests on the simple act of retrieval, something our synapses do. Reclaiming is made biologically possible by our synapses and neuroplasticity, but our will and imagination are doing the work.

We return to our past to create our higher stories from the images we have collected over time. Rich content is there for the finding. It is always time to harness a bit more of our soul. Step 2 of remembrance, reclaiming, is the practice of reminiscence with a purpose—of distillation, of crystallizing your identity around your evocations. We literally do a course correction on our lives with reclaiming, in essence remaking our mental/emotional DNA. We reconstruct the self.

This beyond-the-facts-to-the-latent-power thinking takes us past seeing our yesterdays as a case history and pushes us toward our soul history, our big journey, our brushes and encounters with destiny. This imaginative thinking grabs images by the throat and throttles meaning out of the facts, distilling the truth from the narrative.

---

**Surrending to images and letting them speak to us is how we re-possibilitize. As the authors of our lives, we decide what is most fitting, what helps us to live into the meaning of our most fulfilling, most deserving stories.**

---

Most of us have used reclaiming already, and the challenge, if we want to take more of ourselves to a deeper level, is to use remembrance more often, more deliberately, and more artfully.

In the next chapter, we look at how to work with the compressions.

⤳**Core takeaway idea:** Since our past gives birth to our present, revisiting it thoughtfully is a way to recapture lost parts of us, to rediscover other parts we under-deploy, and to recommit to the values and focal points that make our efforts lasting.

## ▶ STATEMENTS OF INTENT TO ENGAGE THE WILL AND FIRE THE IMAGINATION

I discover my essence by reclaiming the stories that made, are making, and will continue to make me.

I regularly regenerate who I am in my work by tapping the deepest well of myself, a collection of yesterdays drenched in meaning and significant symbols.

I imaginatively explore my yesterdays, seeing the story behind the facts and the myth behind the story.

## ▶ ADDITIONAL OPTIONAL EXERCISE: USING DIALOGUE WITH OTHERS TO RECLAIM

As in recall, bouncing images and stories off your siblings, peers, and coworkers can help to embellish and expand your story. When you recall an event about an important boss with a coworker, and her interpretation varies from yours significantly ("He was a master saboteur and broke my confidence intentionally" versus "He was a provocateur for me and pushed me into talents I had no idea I had"), you are both right. And your boss will have his own version of the story. It is your memory and interpretation of it that carries the meaning, not the event itself. As you revisit these incidents, you have the opportunity to both discover and ascribe new meaning to them. What you may have thought was frozen in your past is really fluid and open to new lessons.

Pick up the phone, post your thoughts on your profile, and let others remind you of their truths and takeaways.

## THE THREE STEPS OF RECLAIMING

| STEP 1 | STEP 2 | STEP 3 |
|---|---|---|
| What is the Level 1 and 2 thinking? | What is it about that image that resonates with me? What are the new Level 2 possibilities? | What does this mean for my work and life currently? |
| *Image*<br>The beer plus the alleluia were so packed with my mom's soul.<br><br>Mom did a lot that year for Lent. What a funny event to have in my mind, and the alleluia was more than a little gesture. | Mom's spirit shone through in that Easter moment with a set of qualities that are worthy to carry on in my life. | I choose to be fun, to enjoy life at at all times, to dedicate myself to the music and joy I was given in the work that I do today. |
| *Image*<br>My football coach and his clipboard: the clipboard with frayed paper and chipped at the corner ever-present, always with notes.<br><br>He helped me to see what I can learn from dedication. | He was so dedicated to us, and his organized approach was a system that made a difference, got the best out of all of us. | I am committed to using organized systematic approaches as a way to excel. His beat-up clipboard is one symbol of the discipline in the upcoming process improvement work. Plus I can use this with soccer practice—as the kids get older, I need to stay ahead of them. |

| Step 1 | Step 2 | Step 3 |
|---|---|---|
| **Image** My first boss told me once, staring at me over his PC, to go after work where "you get to be the glue on a team." I never forgot those words and am not sure if I have applied them all that well. | I keep things cohesive, I am good for teams. I go past participation actually, and this is one of my real gifts. | I need to bring out out the very best in everyone on this do-or-die project. When I really think about it, I get great joy out of bringing all the personalities together on a team. |
| Now do your own | | |
| | | |
| | | |
| List newly recalled images not included in the previous recall chapter. | | |
| What are the images and impacts? | Initial thoughts on why I remember it as important and what it means. | Applying the lessons to now. Early thoughts on implications for me. |
| | | |
| | | |

*Consecrate your demons with the dignity of your attention, leaving no gargoyles in your past, only defiled angels looking for a home.*

—PAT CONROY, *PRINCE OF TIDES*

# Chapter Five: Recast

*Like many serious directors, Christopher Nolan creates movies that play with viewers' minds. One early work was* Memento, *in which the hero desperately searched for the murderer of his wife, and did so with a huge handicap. The hero, Leonard, has clues tattooed on his body and notes crammed everywhere because he is on his quest for justice with a raging case of amnesia.*

*In a diner over a meal, Leonard explains the general limits of memory to a colleague he regularly forgets that he knows: "Memory can change the shape of a room; it can change the color of a car. And memories can be distorted. They're just an interpretation, they're not a record."*

*Later on, alone, thinking about the wife he loved, Leonard describes the specific limits of his memory. "I lie here not knowing . . . how long I've been alone. How am I supposed to heal if I can't . . . feel time?" A profound question.*

IN RECALLING, RECLAIMING, and recasting, we work to feel time and its passage. Especially in recasting, we reinterpret and heal, over and through time.

## ACCENTUATE THE NEGATIVE

As you can tell, I revere the past as a teaching ground. The critics of this approach are right about one thing, however: if we don't jettison the negative lessons from the negative memories and discover their more positive aspects, we may be better off leaving our yesterdays alone. As a reminder, we call the negative events that give rise to the negative memories compressions to describe the reality of how they shrink and limit our potential.

In the last chapter, we spent time harvesting anew some of the great joys and resources that have molded you and your work. In this chapter, we look at the big blocks and trials that caused damage and that you have been overcoming with various degrees of success. Of the three opportunities we have been addressing—identity, potential, and self-direction—this chapter mostly concerns our potential. It is time to focus on the negatives in order to get rid of any negative residual impact. This is where non-paradise did its most non-paradise-type work. To be blunt (and apologies to positive-psychology fans, whose preference for the positive takes what I consider a needed edge off of learning about compressions):

Compressions happen. While we got evoked—groomed and fertilized and provided for—we just as much got mangled and crapped upon and trained away from our gifts. Many parts were prohibited and inhibited and atrophied.

The significant minuses in our lives, the ones you listed in the "Impact on Self" model in chapter 3, placed here for your convenience, are worth special attention. What we do with them deeply affects our attempts to live authentically and do the work we were meant for. We would not have to review compressions if they weren't the source of so many of our limits—our faulty judgment, our bad communication habits, and the blind spots that keep us from being at our best.

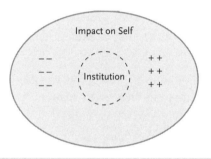

**IMPACT ON SELF TEMPLATE**

So this may be the most important chapter in the book. It may be where we stop the worst of the amnesia. It may be where we can wiggle or blast our way through some inner barrier that is keeping us from getting on with what we are here to do. Here, we take stock of the compressive stories and negative images, reinterpret them to rid ourselves of the poor lessons, and replace these lessons with useful ones. We take our best runs at finding meaning in the tough spots, and by so doing, we reclaim and reintegrate the parts of us that had splintered off.

As you might guess by now, this work will require Level 2 thinking beyond the facts and into the themes and stories behind the images that have grabbed us. The practices we gained in recalling and reclaiming to overcome our amnesia will also help us in recasting.

## GETTING TO KNOW THE MANY NAMES FOR COMPRESSIONS

Compressions are any processes, shortages, or events that limit and shrink our innate potential. They create places in our lifework where we become stuck and ineffective, and these places, as well as the compressions that give birth to them, have many names. We often note a compression indirectly by observing the lack of skilled behavior connected to it. In corporate speak, we refer to a lack of good thinking and its accompanying behaviors as *blind spots* and *derailers*. For those not familiar with leadership-development language, a derailer is a trait or habit that can take you off the track of successful promotions. It is a career killer.

In relationships, the compression shows up when our positive first impression of a talented team member at work gets tempered with further observations—"Oh my, now that I know him, he has issues." Therapists tend to refer to compressions as *complexes* or *wounds*. The term *derailer* is a career-track metaphor, and blind spots are perspectives. A complex is all about neurosis, not that common a term for most. The term *wound*, too negative and therapeutic for general use, does convey soul-level importance. A wound is a piercing of the flesh, one that can go deep and that needs time to heal. It conjures up flesh, blood, and the core vitality of the human spirit.

For our purposes, we will stick with the term *compression*, and you can use the terms that works best for you and your settings. We are after the soul level, however, since that is where the breakthroughs are.

### What's to Lose: Being Captive to Our Experience
### What's to Gain: Our Freedom and Some Wisdom

We all sculpt ourselves, designing our lifework around the material that we were given. What got thrown on the wheel is not much of our choice. But over time, we can mold and shape ourselves. Our taking charge of our self-molding is the source of our freedom. To do this well, we must know and claim our gifts and know our evocations and our compressions. The sculpting is in our hands when we revisit all of our yesterdays, compressions included.

The compressions out of our awareness create rigid behavior, blocking access to our core with its original imagination and magic. Our amnesia enables the blocking, as the thoughts behind the thoughts stay untouched. Pushing the hurt to the unconscious often helps us to get through any hurts for a time, but denying it long term keeps the blocked energy silently active in destructive ways. We become habituated. We don't see our options or allow ourselves to be drawn in new directions. As Paul Hoover wrote, "We drag expensive ghosts through memory's unmade bed."[1]

The big compressions divert us from our highest path in multiple ways, many of them particular to each of us. But here are two common ways:

1. *Compensation.* When we compensate for a past compression, knowingly or unknowingly, we waste our energy. For instance, a person's essential life talent may be teaching or people skills, but because his family was poor and needed money, he gets overfocused on money. The mega-compression of poverty exaggerates the need for making money for decades, even when he has enough in the bank account. I know

an overweight businessman who carries food in his briefcase at all times because he was hungry as a child.

2. *Projection.* Projecting our weaknesses onto others is a second move we make when we have compressions that we have not attended to. We have all seen leaders blame others, wearing no clothes like their emperor predecessor and externalizing problems when they should be looking at how they contributed to the mess they find so blameworthy. How you see *yourself* projecting is the more important question.[2]

## Two More Leaders Who Get It

Let us look at a few examples of compressions well addressed, in which their costs were transformed into the two huge gains that come from accentuating the negatives:

▶ The wisdom from distilling their lessons
▶ The freedom from escaping getting stuck in any long-term impact.

### *Example 1*

When I asked John Pepper, the former CEO and chairman of Procter & Gamble, about his yesterdays, he cited what he wrote in his memoir, *What Really Matters: Service, Leadership, People, and Values*, about coming to grips with alcohol in his family and its damage:

66 As I grew up, I slowly became aware of problems within my family. I could see and sense the relationship deteriorating between my mother and my father. I am sure there were many reasons. . . .

What did become clear to me, sometimes painfully, is that from the earliest years of my childhood, my father, with my mother alongside him, fought the destructive consequences of his alcoholism.[3] 99

Referring to this compression, he told me of the great joys of his evocative education and stellar teachers in prep school and at Yale. He speaks from a place of acquired wisdom, harvested through the power of his yesterdays. In his book, he wrote,

66 Who is wise enough to know the sources of our drives and ambitions, our hopes and fears; the roots of our insecurities and confidences? We know they are rooted in the relationships and experiences that occur early. . . . I was driven to excel. I was your basic overachiever, fueled by my love of learning. And to a degree I was driven, I am sure, to overcome challenges I experienced in my family and insecurities I felt around others.[4] 99

Here, Pepper avoids any flip diagnosis and the mistake of pathologizing his past, choosing instead to see mystery in how his will and personality interacted with the forces and resources surrounding him.

### Example 2

Leaders are everywhere. One of them in my family is Joe Cunningham, a cousin who has spent his life in my hometown, Waukon, Iowa, in the northeast corner of the state. Joe was the city pharmacist and is still one of its major businessmen, as he and his brother Danny developed prominent businesses on Main Street in this county of 20,000 people. Everyone knows Joe and knows his commitment to the community and the families in it.

When I asked him about his past, he talked about the compression of poverty and what he's done with those memories.

> 66 I was raised in a family with four siblings by parents who loved us but who also struggled on the border of poverty. I grew up being poor and not aware of it at the time. I just knew we couldn't have everything everyone else had. As an adult, that upbringing did not cause me to want to be rich or greedy, but it certainly instilled a desire not to be poor. Remembering the financial problems my parents had gives me great empathy for folks who struggle financially. Observing my parents . . . gave me both understanding and an example for the need to be generous in life with all of the blessings God has allowed to come my way.
>
> Being the eldest of five children of a poor family, college was my responsibility, if college was to be in my future. I will never forget the struggle balancing study time against working time so that my grades remained good enough to stay in school and that I had enough money to fund the endeavor. 99

Joe described the most poignant part of this compression and how it motivated him to serve.

> 66 As an adult, I look back and now recognize the hardships my mother endured in life, especially those that faced her as she did her best to feed, clothe, and care for us. I wish that I had had the opportunity to somehow make her life easier. With every good deed and with every act of kindness that I extend to people, I hope that I am somehow repaying or at least acknowledging her sacrifices in life. I did my best to never tarnish the pride she had in who I became. As the oldest child, I found myself reminding my younger brothers and sisters that the five of us kids, and the

pride that mom and dad had in us, were their greatest posses-
sion. I urged them to always remember that and to conduct their
lives accordingly.[5] 🙶

John Pepper, a leader of one of the more powerful corporations in the world, and Joe Cunningham, a leader in a
small community, did the same thing with their compressions. They harvested their lessons with wisdom, and exer-
cised the freedom to go past the facts and circumstances
to the meaning they made. They moved on with their best
contributions.

That is where we are headed.

## WARNING ON TRAUMA

I want to repeat the warning I wrote in the introduction. *If
you have not done any work on serious negative events in
your life, get some professional therapeutic help.* There are
degrees of posttraumatic stress disorder, and that is what
you may be confronting. If you have done some therapeutic work, but you still have some past events that bring up
significant pain, anger, or anxiety, you need to take more
action. Use your network, a neighbor, your minister, a close
colleague; find a therapist and surrender to the healing process that is possible there. No, therapists are not perfect,
and people can use them as a crutch. But without a therapist, revisiting a past trauma may indeed not be the best
route.

We are doing awareness and education work here. This
is not a therapy book.

The distinction between the two can be confusing because
there is a gray area, not a strict boundary, between the two.
The accomplished developmental thinker Jack Mezirow, at

Columbia University, wrote about this boundary/gray area in the challenge of gaining maturing perspectives. "There are wide variations in individual personality that influence one's ability to experience such growth. When serious internal inhibitions impair normal development, an adult may require therapy rather than education."[6]

Who does not have "serious internal inhibitions," and so who does not need therapy at some points in his or her life? (And if you have mood swings that are suspiciously intense, the same advice holds—seek help. Don't let a past bad experience with a therapist, or your friend who has an attitude about it, deter you from trying it again or for the first time. It could be the best thing you ever did for yourself.) But we can do much work on our own as well.

## Balancing the Good and Bad Yields a Workable Truth

It makes sense that much of the power of revisiting our yesterdays is in the places where we got tangled up by the significant compressions we endured. The learning and renewal that are possible when we reflect on the negative images and stories may be enormous, but that does not make recasting easy or simple. All the mistakes in approaching our yesterdays come into play with our compressions. We have amnesia. We avoid/numb out, ignore and erase, hoping the compressions will go away. Or we can victimize, demonize, and pathologize the bad actors and darkness that are normal with the minuses that come with compressions.

At some point, all of us avoid memories, often to some good end, at least for a time. Not doing any vivid recall of a particularly debilitating teacher or boss or significant other, and only sneaking an occasional peek at the memories to see if they are still as painful as we remember them, allows us to stay on our feet, get restabilized, and keep going. But extensive avoiding becomes a problem: the troublesome memory starts to control us even though we may think we have escaped it. Stuffing it is not a long-term strategy.

The reason why stuffing does not work is simple enough: When we stuff a memory, we are stuffing a part of us with it. The memory does not sit idly like inventory in a warehouse. It lives in our heart and has energy. So stuffing a memory means we are cutting ourselves off from ourselves, and the part of us no longer connected will come home to roost, in spite of our efforts to keep it away. In Khaled Hosseini's best-selling novel *The Kite Runner*, the young hero puts it this way: "It's wrong what they say about the past, I've learned, about how you can bury it. Because the past claws its way out."[7]

---

**When we invite a memory back into awareness, we are inviting the part of us we have cut off back home to find its proper place.**

---

So we must stay balanced, given these natural pitfalls. Looking too intensely at the negatives creates a paralysis, a black hole of what is wrong.[8] Even if we don't ever go to that extreme, we all feel the normal effects of too much work with the dark side: becoming hopeless, negative, or even cynical and not realizing it. Given my roots and connections to Catholicism, when the pedophile scandals hit, I found myself saying things like, "Well, is anyone surprised here?" I was taking on a jaded/judging viewpoint, numbing myself from the massive suffering and pain that this sad chapter caused. The data on police officers' losing capacity for empathy over time is more evidence of what work with the broken and compressed can do.

Those who focus too much on their own negatives need to lighten it up and balance it out. Go back and do the previous chapter's exercises on evocations about three more times before you dwell on this chapter.

My experience is that for every one of us who is overfocused on the compressions, there are two of us with learned amnesia who skip over the compressions as unnecessary. They see it as a weakness, or an indulgence, or a waste of time to talk about bad and limiting experiences from their past.

---

**We pass over our compressions—the mistakes of ignoring, avoiding, and numbing out—because to think about them is to admit that something is wrong. This is simply not true. It is normal to have some compressed, less-than-stellar parts of us, born of our past; and to work on them is a sign of strength, not weakness.**

---

We all know people who, for whatever reasons, have not taken on the tough tasks of confronting their compressions and who have read one too many positive-mental-attitude books. I once knew a saleswoman in her mid-30s who was a devoted mom with a newborn, and she said to me in desperation, "Why aren't my positive-mental-attitude practices working anymore?" She was in need of some new, deeper approaches, ones that add depth when positive thinking can't. It became obvious that her newborn provided an opportunity for recalling where her priorities originated, and not only an occurrence for positive self-talk.

---

**A balanced effort yields you the truth, and reality by itself can set you free. Balance helps you to claim those core gifts on the positive side while acquiring the empathic toughness that comes from head-on confrontations with the compressions and hurts.**

---

## WORKAHOLICS AND MORE: CULTURALLY ENABLED AND COMPRESSED

Many successful people escape a wounding compression from their yesterdays by sticking to a strategy that worked when they were young—hard work. This strategy, aided by amnesia and by the good intention of staying positive, often leads to workaholic extremes, a well-disguised culturally accepted addiction. Overwork can mean major underdevelopment of the capacity for intimacy, like our group of men from chapter 1 who would rather have had their nails pulled out than have a conversation involving feelings. We ruin our relationships with spouses and kids through the emotional absenteeism that comes with workaholism, all the while offering a beautiful explanation of how dedicated we are as providers.

Overwork was me for quite some time; here is the back story. In my family, our parents subtly pressured my older sister, Elaine, and me to get all A's in school. As a result, I thought I was more lovable when I was performing well.

This did not translate well into my adult life in many ways—overachieving to a fault, I kept setting impossible goals and not savoring life or keeping enough balance.

Now for the all-important images that burned the story in my memory, a story that my mom told for decades: When my younger sister, Mary Ann, saw her first report card as a first-grader, she pointed to an A and asked, "Is that a straight A?" and Mom laughed at the cuteness of her question. Can you hear, and feel, the compression in that simple verbal image, "straight A"? Straight A was the expectation, and it meant we were loved, and we were even *more* loved with a slight condition of performing at a very high level. These kids didn't just have good report cards; they got straight A's all the time, no matter what.

All of us in my family—my parents and later my sisters and me as adults—would entirely miss the compression factor that Elaine and I faced. Mom would tell her story, and we would all laugh and move on. I had sentimentalized my past and had no clue how to connect the costs of my overwork, which gets disguised as dedication and other good things, with "straight A's." I just kept setting unreasonable stretch goals and putting in massive hours.

Long ago, through recalling and recasting, I came to terms with this story. I had to, because I was still overworking and not savoring enough of life (why, at age 45, did I still want to please somebody?). With as much progress as I have made, however, I may never fully override my tendency to overwork. The habits don't disappear so much as they grow weaker, and at best I can manage them well by staying aware.

But "Straight A" is more than a story for workaholics. It is for all of us: you may have faced some other condition for acceptance.

As I told the story, did you start thinking of yourself a few decades ago, a fourth-grade or high school or young adult version of you trying to get hugs and acceptance, trying to feel competent and worthy as you encountered life? From the nods I get when I tell this story to groups, there are many like me, unable to break the habit of over-effort. But for you, it may have been not asserting your point of view, or never getting angry, or pretending that you were perfect, or a thousand other mistaken tactics whose origins you forgot long ago. We take these learned tactics as part of our personality—"It is just my nature to drive for perfection." It may be, and it may just as well be a learned behavior stemming from a long-forgotten compression.

The amnesia we all learn and our desire not to dwell on the negative prevent us from exploring the originating compressions. We can escape thinking about our compressions indefinitely if we work at it. But we can't escape our shortcomings. You get feedback at work that you are a bad listener, and you have been told this 20 times and don't change. Or you avoid giving feedback to a teammate who really needs it because you get tight in the chest when you give tough news. Or you don't give your kids much time but you give people at work the time they need.

While we may be able to escape thinking about the past, it is impossible to escape the negatives of certain patterns that are not working. This is where the work of recasting comes in. If we review the negative stories from our past with an eye toward getting help with something we are stuck on today, we can make tremendous headway.

As with the positive images of evocation, this is how we do the work on compressions: going back to the images.

We steadily move into truer forms of our lifework when
we see the past fully, with a keen eye for both the gifts
and good luck and the downers and lousy fortune. Then,
armed with the truth, we refuse to be limited by our
yesterdays. We choose anew our attitudes, our operating-
system thoughts, and our ways of being.

I got better when I admitted the negatives of this overwork compression and saw its meaning. My work got truer,
more powerful, more my own and not somebody else's,
when I confronted, by simply admitting it, the whole story
(funny elements included) of straight A's and other negatives in my generally positive yesterdays. When I allowed
myself to feel the anger/alienation/sadness of being social-
ized, of creating a provisional life out of some damaging
tactics, I got better at living my real life with healthier ones.
I stopped the endless push for earning love through performance and decided that I could just receive love on its own
terms. Accepting the damage I had incurred as real and not
minimal helped me to move into a more authentic voice,
not the quasi-artificial sculpted one of the professional version of me that I had fabricated to make a living.

Now it is your turn.

### RECAST EXERCISE: REINTERPRETING THE COMPRESSIONS

As with reclaiming, recasting is not primarily about historical accuracy. It is about meaning and growth that come
through courage and imagination. Once again, we approach
our yesterdays and their images with wonder, without

rancor for the villains or pity for ourselves. We recall and recast through our willingness to take the broadest attitude of learning that we can, and to take what emerges to heart.

You may wonder how much time you should spend reflecting on your compressions. It is different for each of us, of course. The only real answer is: as much as you need to. You can bring on some natural melancholy with recasting, so don't stay too long at any one setting in this work. If you tend to get immobilized by the negative, then briefer journeys, but many of them, may be better for you. For the positive oriented, my advice is to stay here longer than you want to and are used to. Recasting compressions into new lessons is truly inspirational, and it may be something you need to practice.

Finally, don't follow these steps rigidly—or any others, for that matter. Your awareness and imagination, naming the old truth and recasting new ones, are what we are after.

### Guidelines

Here are the three steps of recasting:

1. Identify and analyze the impacts of the compressions.
2. Recast their meaning by unfreezing and updating them with your wisdom.
3. Apply the new lessons to current settings.

### Step 1: Identify and Analyze the Compression Stories and Images and Their Impacts

We can start with the minuses of the diagrams and stories from the work in chapter 3, "Recall," either the oval with minuses or the third column in the chart. The stories about school and religion and early bosses and all the other institutions that compressed you are the places to start. These already-known stories and images will likely hold previous explanations. They are probably the ones in need of reinterpretation and updating. Use the ideas below on unfreezing and the idea flow from the chart below to get you going, which is also available on my website at www.johnpschuster .com/thepowerofyourpast.

Expand from this, your original list, when you are ready to do more recasting, and include stories now coming to mind or ones you missed or avoided in your first run at recalling.

### Step 2: Recast Their Meaning by Unfreezing and Updating with Your Wisdom

Unfreezing allows the new lessons to emerge from the compressions. As the word implies, we take a fixed image and make it liquid and malleable by asking ourselves questions like the following:

▶ What is the image a symbol of—an attitude, an experience, a dilemma?
▶ Why *that* image—is it loaded with a back story worth rethinking?
▶ What new thoughts about the image are possible? What other ways can I look at it?
▶ What is the image trying to teach me? Where does my imagination take this?

When we have habituated explanations of our compressions, we often victimize and demonize (yes, bad guys and gals did bad stuff to poor me, but that was then). Spend time bringing up new details, and noticing new feelings, thoughts, and possibilities. Have real compassion for yourself. What tender and innocent parts of you could not protect themselves from the forces that did the damage? What was the damage? Have you let yourself feel the anger long enough that it eventually dissipates? What have you overcome and strengthened though your maturity and courage? What lessons in life can come from this compression?

Don't push here. And don't give in to the anger or sadness, but allow it. It is better to dwell, ponder, stand in awe of your life and the amazing process of healing and growing to wholeness. Then the insights emerge. You are imagining and evoking, not extracting or forcing. As in the earlier exercises, sharing the stories with your spouse, siblings, and peers can spark your imagination and unfreeze those perspectives.

### Step 3: Apply to Your Current Situation with Imagination

Once you have new inklings of possibilities, or new rushes of huge insights, look at how the issues in your current life can be addressed with the new wisdom that your best adult self can bring to your younger compressions.

### ▶ Summary

Compressions affect our ability to truly express who we are and to do the work we are meant to do. Since we are walking museums of the artifacts of our identities, the images we inherited from our joyous and broken yesterdays, reconsidering these images is the way to reset our course.

We don't want to invent ourselves, or choose our lifework, out of the mishmash of images and ideas brought on

## The Three Steps of Recasting

| Step 1 | Step 2 | Step 3 |
|---|---|---|
| Images or stories I remember. Analyze the images and name the impacts. | Recast their meanings by unfreezing and updating with wisdom. | Apply the new possible meanings to the current situation. |
| What are the impacts to this point? | What occurs to me now as new lessons from a mature perspective? What possibilities are there? | What does this mean for my work and life currently? |
| Parental performance pressure; the impact of this pressure created self-destructive strategies to win approval through overwork. | My folks were proud of us, and I realize how love-based this parental pressure was—to help us use our potential in the world and to apply ourselves. | I can pass the lesson on to my kids, and now my grandkids, of how to apply oneself but not get caught up with self-worth. |
| *Image*<br>My mom laughing, telling the "Straight A" story regularly, and our laughing along because no one had made the connection to overwork for decades. | *Recast*<br>I see now, however, that I don't have to do the impossible to win acceptance. | I work with executive workaholics on pacing and their underlying need to win, or however they got compressed into it—for money or status, or approval.<br><br>I help clients to better relate to the people in their lives at work and at home through improved presence. |

| Step 1 | Step 2 | Step 3 |
|---|---|---|
| My first boss used his treatment of me as an example of his toughness. The impact was raging low confidence for some time.<br><br>**Image**<br>A weekly chewing in his office on my projects that was subtle—no yelling, but biting. "Is this the best you can do?" | I avoided this memory for some time but not its effects.<br><br>**Recast**<br>I eventually had enough successes to override this bad start, and I vowed that I would never break somebody else's confidence with sarcasm, which I was once pretty good at. | I have ample opportunity right now, on my volunteer board and in my job.<br><br>I can smell lack of confidence across the room now and will always try to find a way to help build confidence for whoever doesn't have it. |
| Your examples here —below and on a separate sheet. | | |
| | | |
| | | |
| | | |

by the misinformed others we once had to rely on. Level 1 thinking on our compressions is a dead end of facts. We must use our Level 2 thinking to learn how to use these mental/emotional bumps and bruises. Even the trauma of big injuries can lead us to positive ends that align us with our calling. If we work with them well, they give us the strength and wisdom to choose new options.

We are not attempting to create a perfect past here, only to limit and override our stuck points with new choices. We don't eliminate our blind spots. We will derail ourselves again and again. Perfection is not the goal, but authenticity and alignment are, and recasting our compressions toward a working truth forms the basis of ongoing resilience and recovery.

When we deny our compressions, we are doomed to live a false version of ourselves. When we try to forget our compressions with the accepted amnesia tactics, we are doomed to live a shallow version of ourselves.

We come ever closer to our truth through recasting the compressions that hold the energy for who we are. We examine our major compressions for residual damage—thoughts behind the thoughts that block us through false past interpretations—so that we can be free to be ourselves. We will never track down all the compressions, nor is it important to, but we do enough recalling and recasting to make sure that we are ourselves and not somebody else's version of us.

⤳ *Core takeaway idea:* **By confronting the negatives from our past creatively, we recast their lessons in ways that expand our stories and contribute mightily to our capacity to do our lifework.**

## ▶ Statements of Intent to Engage the Will and Fire the Imagination

By confronting the negative events of my past, I can grow in wisdom and extract meaning that otherwise was not available to me.

It is not what happened in my past that determines my lifework; it is how I choose to learn from my past and the choices I make.

The inevitable compressions I have absorbed teach me empathy for others.

*Memory believes before knowing remembers.*
*Believes longer than recollects, longer than*
*knowing even wonders.*

—William Faulkner, *Light in August*

~~~~~~~~~~~~~~~~~~~~~~~~~~~~~~~~~~~~~~~~~~~~~~~~~~~~~~~~~~

# PART III
## Channeling the Power of Your Past

THE SHORTER CHAPTERS in this section are advanced applications of the ideas on how to use your past. We have explored learning from our history by reimagining the stories and images we all carry within. These final discussions and exercises provide more frameworks and opportunities for important learning.

If you instead just jumped into this section, enjoy the chapters for the questions they raise and the models they explore.

The heavy lifting we addressed in part 2 leads to the refined applications in this concluding section. We look at what it means to be unique in the world, to say no to its shallowness, and yet to stay healthily and even productively connected to it. Our past can help us in this most crucial act of balance, courage, and discernment. And we end with the mystery and usefulness of healthy suffering as a means to expand our capacity through both our past compressions and our current events of loss.

*The historical experience is not one of staying in the present and looking back. Rather it is one of going back into the past and returning to the present with a wider and more intense consciousness of the restrictions of our former outlook. We return with a broader awareness of the alternatives open to us and armed with a sharper perspective with which to make our choices. In this manner it is possible to loosen the clutch of the dead hand of the past and transform it into a living tool for the present and the future.*

—WILLIAM APPLEMAN WILLIAMS, *THE CONTOURS OF AMERICAN HISTORY*

# Chapter Six: Answering the Big Question: When to Say Yes and No

*In an amnesia-themed story by Don DeLillo,* The Names, *a character describes the social fabric: "All of this we choose to forget. We devise a countersystem of elaborate forgetfulness . . . but the experience is no less deep because we chose to forget it."*[1]

*Collective-amnesia themes are not as common as themes about individuals with memory loss, but they still show up often. A whole city or tribe or planet forgets its origin and its nature. As the story unfolds, the clues to its history emerge, and the shock of remembering can be a horror. In the Charlton Heston movie* Soylent Green, *our disguised source of food, due to planetary overcrowding, had become other humans. But if we are mindful of our memories, the recovery from amnesia may be a liberation and a link to the society's truest, noblest nature.*

*Elaborate forgetfulness can lead us down paths that serve us poorly. We need to take great care to prevent our amnesia from forging a countersystem that works against what we are here to do.*

155

OUR STORIES DEFINE us. Our stories confine us. Memories provide fuel for reinventing and rediscovering ourselves. Recalling, reclaiming, and recasting knead our memories for what we need to learn and what we hope to change. While memories themselves are important, remembrance, an act of amnesia-reducing recollection and reflection, is more important still. When we revisit our history as a more experienced and wiser person, we can remake ourselves. We choose richer interpretations than the simpler, less nuanced, sometimes downright mistaken conclusions of our younger selves.

In this chapter, we take a look at how to choose between accepting non-paradise and its messages when necessary, and defying those messages by making our own path-less-taken choices. Of the three opportunities we have been addressing—identity, potential, and self-direction—this chapter mostly focuses on self-direction.

## WHY SAY YES TO SOME THINGS, NO TO OTHERS

As social beings, we need to belong to the world we were born into, as flawed as it may be, or else we have no moorings or home. We surrender, in part, to the version of non-paradise we experienced. And like all truths we have explored, the polar opposite contains value. Each of us also has a raging drive to stand apart from the world as it is and to stand for and live out something better. In large measure, learning about evocation, compression, and remembrance is in service to balancing these two drives—to explore both our uniqueness and our place in the everydayness of the world. We undergo a lifelong holy and fully practical effort to take our gifts and apply them in a way that no one else can.

The earlier versions of us have two choices when we react to the compressions and evocations that surround us: we can accept the explanations for our experience as our own (adopt others' thinking, as inadequate as it may be), or reject the explanations (and make up our own mind, as clueless as we may be). The first choice is to integrate and the second choice is to differentiate. We go through life bouncing between these two poles, thus creating who we are and what we do.

Examples abound, of course. Let's look at two—our choices of career and religious practice.

### Integration
Absorb life as we find it and accept the explanation as to why.

*I am an accountant because I tested well in math, I can make money, and my parents thought it was a good, steady profession.*

*I am a Methodist because my family is Methodist, it seems complete as a spiritual approach, and I love my family.*

### Differentiation
Reject the prevailing guidance and find another way, crafting or discovering a new explanation.

*I am an accountant because I love the profession, even though my mom and dad, both artists, thought I should be a jazz pianist.*

*I can't settle on a religion to choose, and I love my parents' Methodist authentic life.*

The reality is usually not as succinct as the above examples, and we spend much of our life in the gray area between choices, trying to sort out the influences we want to go with from those we want to swim against. Differentiation can also lead to another place—living with the anxiety of not having an adequate explanation, at least not yet. We may know that the explanations we have been given are not for us, and may be either confident, even with the anxiety, or daunted by the journey to find some answers that work for us.

This polar lens of differentiation/integration is a useful one for our work with remembrance. As we were given the gift of evocations and the challenge of compressions, we can use reclaiming and recasting to strike a useful balance between differentiation and integration in our lifework.

## TWO MORE LEADERS WHO GET IT

In the interviews I conducted for this book, I found many examples of differentiating and integration. Here are two of them.

### Example 1

Cheryl Kravitz, former regional head of the National Conference for Community and Justice (formerly the National Conference of Christians and Jews), tells the story of how she differentiated in high school, where it led her, and how an image from the cover of *Newsweek* followed her.

❝ Martin Luther King marched through our neighborhood [in Chicago] in 1965. And it was during that time period that the National Conference of Christians and Jews was running an essay contest. They wanted to talk of civil rights. I was in high school and I wrote an essay for that . . . I felt that people should be able to live together, survive and thrive. And I won the contest. And on the front cover of *Newsweek* was a picture of Martin

Luther King and his marchers being stoned by a bunch of young men who were actually in my English class in that high school.

And the years passed, and much later there was a job opening as executive director of the National Conference of Christians and Jews for the D.C. region. And so I wrote them and said I'd written this essay, and one of the lines I remembered distinctly in the essay was that when I grew up, I was going to do whatever work I could in civil rights and here's my chance, and they hired me. . . .

Some years ago, I was in Memphis where Dr. King was killed, and the memorial to him is like a civil rights museum, and you go decade by decade through the civil rights movement. In the room that's dedicated to the '60s, you have that same picture from Newsweek. It's like the past, the present, and future were all in the same room. I had no idea at the time, in '65, that I would make good on that promise so many years later.[2] 🙙

## *Example 2*

The name Jorma Kaukonen is revered by most guitar players. He played for the Jefferson Airplane, not a bad start to a music career, and many know him more for his later work in acoustic blues in the still-touring Hot Tuna. Jorma has made a lot of great music, has escaped the dark side of the music scene, and now, when not performing, runs a thriving guitar camp, Fur Peace Ranch, in the Appalachian hills of southeastern Ohio. He tells stories of early peer pressure to unhealthily integrate (it is not confined to work settings), and carries the images of the conversations and people that sourced his later commitments to teaching and playing his way.

🙙 You know, John, when we were younger, and it still is, smoking was cool. . . . Drinking was a rite of passage, it was a way to becoming an adult. And so me and my buddies started drinking when we were young teenagers, you know. And that we didn't get in a lot of trouble or kill ourselves was just a miracle. The drugs came later . . . that sort of outsider thing that I think me and some of my friends found attractive . . . I don't know what the deal is—I don't know if that's something intrinsically tied to being an artist or not or if that's just a great excuse to party. I was a dumb ass some of the time when I was younger, but the music helped me stay centered and it sort of carried me through.

One pivotal moment was in early 1960 when I was in Antioch College in Yellow Springs, Ohio, and I met Ian Buchanan. He was a friend of Reverend Gary Davis's, and he taught me to finger-pick, basically. And he turned me on to a bunch of the guys that really became sort of my, for lack of a better word, muses, in a really profound kind of way. Now I don't know what it was about gospel music—my mom was Jewish and my dad was Lutheran, and there was really no religion in our house when I grew up, but there was gospel music. And why that was, I don't know. And when I started to learn how to play some of that myself—spiritual music, really—it was a defining moment in my life. Because I wasn't playing rock 'n' roll then, I was just playing this very traditional, finger-style guitar that at the time was mostly played by black guys.

I moved to California in 1962—I was going to school and my father was sending me some money, God bless him, every month—somebody offered me a job teaching guitar at this music store. One of my folk music buddies said, "You've got to do this. You get three bucks an hour." I went, "Wow, three bucks an hour." So I started to teach and I began to think about what I was doing. The little room—we had two teaching rooms downstairs in this tiny little music store and the teaching rooms I doubt were any more than, I don't know, 6 to 8 feet square. And I really began to think about what I do today in a much more primitive way. . . . I really enjoyed passing that stuff on. And I think that . . . what I started to do in this little music store in California in 1962 was really the roots of what I do today.[3] 🙺

Escaping prejudice for Cheryl, succumbing to social pressure for Jorma but letting the evocations of his early teacher carry him through the bad parts—the images that both hold from early adulthood held a definite power. With remembrance, the images eventually foster meaning and verification for their lifework. Their legacy spins out from encounters not fully understood when they were younger, but harvested by the wiser versions of who they became.

## WHY SAYING NO IS IMPORTANT

We have all known people who don't do very well living the differentiation/integration polarity, losing either their soul or their effectiveness, or both, when they plant themselves too far toward one of the poles.

The trap is to get stuck in compliance or defiance, with an on/off button for our responses to non-paradise. Black or white, yes or no, may feel good for a time, but regular hyper-pure responses push us too far one way. Remembrance allows us to create more opportunities for wisdom and new combinations of choices.

When doing leadership and community development, my colleagues and I create learning experiences that promote differentiating and saying no to the pressures to conform. (This is where the life-line exercise I illustrated in chapter 2 fits in.) The reason is simple: the environment. Social pressure most commonly drives and rewards conformity. Leadership shrivels when conformity is in the air. While it varies greatly even within subgroups of the overall enterprise, the pressure is hugely on the side of integration into the culture, even when there is an expressed value to innovate. Small businesses can be the exceptions to this (or they can be worse, with a strong owner and compliant employees), but most often, the larger the enterprise, the more integration seeps in and saturates.

The integration messages dovetail with people's efforts to advance in the enterprise. This is a toxic mix. Advancing is fine, of course, but the social drumbeat to fit in is often overwhelming for those who are going full-tilt boogie into their careers and still carry inside the bad fruit of compressions they have yet to recast into more holistic views. The beat whispers into our ears things like the following:

- ► Work long hours—we'll show you how long.
- ► Don't battle this sacred cow; the senior vice president won't allow it.
- ► Wear these clothes.
- ► Have loyalty to our practices—they are working.
- ► *You* are the leader here, so model all that is acceptable.

The need to integrate is legitimate—it connects us to our colleagues and the culture, creating cohesion.

---

**But the rewards for fitting in, especially when tied to those well-disguised compression-originated thoughts, will drive us to superficially adapt, to follow the crowd, and to lose our soul.**

---

Our long-ago-forgotten compressions create the thoughts; the hidden, powerful Level 2 thoughts behind the thoughts; the ones that collude with the withering collective whispers. Together they are a bad combination for losing our essence and staying on the surface of our lives. It goes something like this:

Work long hours—we'll show you how long.
*I have always valued really hard work, and my family understands the price of success.*

Don't battle this sacred cow; the senior vice president won't allow it.
*I see why she cuts that corner; it really doesn't matter. I would too.*

Wear these clothes.
*I like our dress code—why think otherwise?*

Have loyalty to our practices—they are working.
*Sure, we could do better with real conflict of ideas, but why bother? The work is getting done.*

You are the leader here!
*I am the smartest dude in the room, as usual.*

The outward pressure to perform and conform combines with and amplifies the inner drive to succeed. The result is that we watch our unique work life shrivel, and our feet start to hurt from those small shrinking shoes that Jung talked about. We sweat the trivial and avoid our own courage:

Can I have a dialogue with my colleagues at this meeting, or do I slick up the process with a PowerPoint presentation?

*Shall I pursue this issue or is it going to piss off the board?*

Much leadership development work is about reinstilling the courage to be ourselves after our intense, sustained runs at business and career goals demanded some compromise and conformity, and even self-damage. This is the counter-system of forgetfulness—amnesia over what we are really here for—that we must guard against.

**We need to regularly review how much we have stayed true to our singular path of meaning.**

I coached a Brit by the name of Nick Hill, the CEO of a global manufacturing company who pushed himself hard for three years to create and execute a bold new strategy. He made his company better in all ways, regularly confronted by feedback that his brand as a leader was that he was something of a renegade. Then, while in his early 50s, and after much thought, he focused on the social-responsibility feature of the business; started the Planet Water Foundation; and left his position to others who wanted to be CEO more than he did. He claimed one of his big passions, using technology to alleviate the effects of bad water in poor villages around the world.

Like Nick Hill, after a lengthy campaign for results, leaders need to get centered again in their values and aspirations. With a coach, perhaps, or a good boss or peer who cares about our development, we look for those thoughts behind the thoughts, any evocations that need reclaiming, or any self-eroding practices from a compression that need to be eliminated or recast.

For a sizable group of us, becoming grossly dissatisfied with the life of fitting in is an important step in answering our call to be authentic.

I remember a lively conversation with a teacher in which he expressed his rage at the way many teachers are exploited: long hours and low pay and too much empty talk from leadership about values. He came down from his anger to a more reasoned place, but the instinct to be dissatisfied for a time served him in his drive to both find himself and accommodate himself to a profession and a calling.

Whether we are at work, at home, in the community, or playing guitar, if we overdo integration, we suppress our individuality. Our task, then, is to rekindle the belief that there indeed is a singular life all our own that we can forge even as we address the mundane chores of everyday roles in our families, communities, and careers. Those of us in the midst of career building and testing the limits of our gifts are generally freed up and ennobled by the counter-message to differentiate, to reconsider our thoughts behind the thoughts and core values and the impact we want to make.

## WHEN TO SAY YES TO NON-PARADISE

And what about lessons for those who have gone too far in the opposite direction? Yes, on the other side, some of us overdifferentiate. We succeeded in blocking out the social pressure but in the process may have become the one who also has rejected social commitments. Being compressed to get a degree, we dropped out. Being groomed to take over the family business, we move to Fiji. We may well have a soul but too little impact on the world because we don't have connection points. People refer to us as the black sheep. We read poetry on the beach and may have beautifully developed hearts and minds, but we have not made enough commitments to a profession or a person or an institution. We may have rejected the social pressure and stayed pure and spirited, but rendered ourselves ineffective and powerless.

I know this territory. In separating from my family pressures in my 20s, I showed my family that I did not have to conform. I joined a cult. I will have to write about that some day—it was not my most elegant choice. I recovered quickly enough and never fully left life's mainstream, but such a drastic move grew my compassion for the overdifferentiated souls among us, as I understand how strong the drive to defy the pressure from non-paradise to conform really is.

With the overdifferentiated, if I am in a position to provide some guidance, I walk down a different path than the leadership work in the organization settings I mentioned above. I might use questions like the following, depending on the particulars:

- ▶ How would getting a job and keeping it give form to your purpose?
- ▶ How might knowing more about economics and the world in general be of help? What would it mean to take out a mortgage?
- ▶ What benefits for staying in a relationship or a career would come to you and others?

There is a place for mystics and visionaries in the world, those who live ahead of their time and hold a view from the mountaintops. But full-time, highly differentiated mystics are rare. Thoreau may have gone to Walden Pond to avoid living a life of quiet desperation, but even he wrote about it and integrated in his own way.

We all need to be self-authoring in order to be fulfilled, and we must all work to stay grounded in the world, but only to a point. Neither misfits who are too singular to be heard nor "normal" people who unknowingly work at being unoriginal can have their best impact on non-paradise.

## CHOOSING YOUR YES/NO MOVE

As you think about your work life now, consider whether you face the choice to differentiate, and to discover and deepen your voice. Or perhaps you are being invited by your life, which does speak to you, to attach to something and fit in. You may need to learn the power of making a commitment to a person or an institution or a process. It may be a new attachment, more aligned with who you are now in your updated form. Your inner self may have moved ahead, but your old commitments on the outside may not have caught up.

Integrating is the easier choice in life for most of us and therefore the more common problem. It takes less work and risk to full-out integrate and absorb the world's explanations for why things are the way they are.

---

**The whole thrust behind the phrase "a well-adjusted person" is that the don't-make-any-waves life—to accept it all, and get the education and the job and the spouse you are expected to get—will settle you into the work and life that will make you happy.**

---

A midlife crisis can happen to any adult, young or old. It is the wake-up call from the core of you, the soul, to the rest of you; it tells you that the compromising that comes with fitting in is too high a price. Each yes may be another pound of flesh, and there is only so much of that to go around. Our discontent is our soul saying, "No more of this, please; we can't keep bargaining away our uniqueness with more easy yeses." Boredom and the urge for newness are signals that it is a good time to listen, to deepen, to review our yesterdays for clues. They are not signals to fall in love with a shiny new car or the gardener, or to increase our DVD viewing. Those are the types of diversions that only postpone the inevitable meeting we must have with ourselves.

That meeting includes knowing our yesterdays through the process of recalling, reclaiming, and recasting.

►**Summary**

The wiser version of us emerges when we reclaim what is ours from those earlier images, like Cheryl Kravitz and her civil rights essay, or Jorma Kaukonen in the tiny room in the music store in California. And it emerges when we reject the compressions that once made sense ("I like going to my mom's alma mater") or were too hard to go against when we did not have the resources or experience ("If you even think about not going into medicine, you can pay your own tuition").

Knowing whether to jump in and get grounded or step out and differentiate is often the key to taking the next step in our life. If we are already successful in life as defined by our career and financial well-being, if we have already been senior vice president of overhead somewhere, then pursuing meaning and contribution is our best option.

▷*Core takeaway idea:* **Our quest into our past yields unique gifts that help us to stand apart from the world, while we apply those gifts to change the world from which we must never fully separate.**

►**Statements of Intent to Engage the Will and Fire the Imagination**

I strike the balance of being in the world and living my truth; I relish and ride the tension.

My unique history of potential, evocations, and compressions provides me with a unique story that only I can live and that can serve the planet.

I make money and have a career and relationships that matter. I fit in well. I pay no attention to the world's common pressure to conform. I am all my own person.

▶**EXERCISE**

*Questions for Balancing Your Yeses and Nos*
"What have I done this day, this hour, that feeds my core, my most real self?" is the common question of our soul. It is a spiritual version of "What have you done for me lately?" Staying true to ourselves requires a lifetime of answering this question, a balance of little and big rebellions and of the easy and difficult agreements to staying part of, but in important ways distinct from, non-paradise.

FOR THE OVERDIFFERENTIATED
Have you

- ▶ surrendered your will to the will of a friend or spouse or boss?
- ▶ read a John Grisham novel, gone to a pop movie, or done some totally ordinary thing and just enjoyed it?
- ▶ gone back to a traditional religion and found its beauty and truth?
- ▶ stayed with a job, even through the boring parts?
- ▶ stayed with a person, even through his/her boring parts?

### For the Overintegrated

Have you

- ▶ made an unpopular decision that created some heat?
- ▶ done something for yourself with food or clothing or music, other than buy what everyone else does?
- ▶ gone to a coffeehouse populated by the fringe?
- ▶ dared to voice an opinion that diverged big time from that of someone who likes to be agreed with?

### For All

Have you

- ▶ recalled an image from your history that points in a new direction, giving you energy, even if it does not make total sense in the context of your life? How can you entertain this image for a while to see what it is telling you?

*What*
*Do sad people have in*
*Common?*

*It seems*
*They have all built a shrine*
*To the past*

*And often go there*
*And do a strange wail and*
*Worship.*

*What is the beginning of*
*Happiness?*

*It is to stop being*
*So religious*

*Like*

*That.*
—Hafiz, "Stop Being So Religious"

# Chapter Seven: Using Suffering to Grow

*Near the beginning of Dickens's novel* Nicholas Nick-leby, *in a long discussion of memory and happiness, one gentleman says, "Memory, however sad, is the best and purest link between this world and a better." This short assertion describes the power of our past for connecting us to our more ideal world. That is why amnesia is the enemy, and while it may block what is sad for a time, it stunts the growth that can come from working with the sadder side of life.*

## Your Discontent and Suffering Have Meaning

We have described the ways to use courage and imagination for making our memories a source for reinventing ourselves. In the previous chapter, we formulated mental frameworks for staying true to ourselves in the midst of past compressions and social pressures not to. And finally, here, we look at a universal human experience that can shrink us or make our path more meaningful, depending on how we handle it. We look at the experience of loss.

The biggest secret about remembrance, and maybe its biggest payoff, is that when we recall and recast, we turbocharge our growth by learning how to creatively suffer. Creative suffering expands our presence because fewer dynamics have control over us and because we enlarge our hearts.

Losses are a type of compression—the ones not stemming from social institutions, which have been our emphasis until now. A loss is a compression that has the potential to shrink us because we have extended parts of our identities and souls into work, or relationships, or patterns of being, and now those parts of us are gone.

The loss of a career we loved, a friend of 25 years, even a soulful practice like running that is now gone because of an injury—these losses take some of us away with them. We say good-bye to cherished parts of us. Like earlier compressions—inheriting a nasty racial bias from an otherwise loving parent, or a simple lack of resources when you could have used them—losses throughout our lives take away a form of self-expression or potential.

Soulfully confronting these losses, which I will refer to as suffering, is a mindset we can all use to help us grow past our current limits. Suffering is heartfelt distress, emotional/mental/spiritual upset, and even anguish that we consciously endure. It can be caused by physical pain, but it is not physical pain by itself. It is not suffering if we are not conscious of it. Nor is it suffering if we stay shallow and indulge ourselves in complaining over the small stuff— "Oh, I am so frustrated with my bad hair . . . of all days!"

## The Small May Be a Clue to the Significant

Shallow, bad-hair-day-type anxiety, a kind of fretting and irritability, is very often tied to deeper issues of suffering. Jung said that "neurosis is suffering that has not discovered its meaning yet." An exaggerated fit over bad hair might be tied to a deep sense of inadequacy. An emotional spinout over the kids' messing up the family room may be tied to feeling hopeless and out of control in your career. We need to always look for the patterns where the little behavior is evidence of the deeper struggle, the one we are worthy of.

I noticed one of my executive clients telling stories with cynical endings about her boss. This client used to have better things to say about her boss, but now his shortcomings were always at play. No one story was belittling, and they were often about small interactions, but taken together, a pattern emerged. I pointed this out to her, and in our dialogue, she came to the conclusion that the cynicism was really a signal of a deep disappointment. She had let the little disappointments eat at her; she had gotten disheartened (think about the power of that word). An old pattern of resorting to cynicism to protect her from disappointments kept her from doing her best work. She was not reaching out often enough, in the best of her motivating and uplifting moods, to her huge sales force of over 10,000. So after the conversation, we knew what to confront and how she had to better suffer, and endure, many of the de-motivating features, and there were many, of her boss.

*Confronting our little neurotic upsets and patterns, linking them to the compressions worthy of our attention, and moving on from them as we recast and create new practices is like taking spiritual steroids. There is nothing faster or stronger for our growth than digging into our suffering with intention. This steroid is legal but requires courage.*

Most of us would prefer to have a loss-free life, and if we have some good luck, we may be able to avoid big losses (your team losing in the finals almost qualifies, but not quite) for much of the first half of life. Hormones and youth generally help for several decades to keep the "gain train" fully on the track—more kids, more promotions, bigger houses, more experiences. The way it should be. (Although by now you know that, in my view, all of us with this kind of success still have compressions to recast.) But eventually, the switch gets thrown and the gain train takes a ride on the loss track, sometimes in surprising ways and always in spite of our best efforts. The loss may be an event, or it could be a nonevent as vexing as the fading away of meaning in a specific job that until now has provided just that.

If we do own up to our internal misery and distress, the kind that loss triggers, one approach that can work for a time, on the minor losses, is to simply stop whining when it is time to move on. "Oh, why did my boss pass me over for that assignment I so-o-o deserved, oh why?" most likely calls for, before too long, a good "Enough already!" "Chill out!" or "Get a grip and stop wallowing!"

On the true losses, however, halting the whining is not enough, because it is not whining. It is real anguish. Regularly cutting off the pain, which we can get very good at, is even dangerous. It leads to the advanced numbing-out strategies of seeking relief in the shallowness of cultural addictions—empty TV, careless consumption, or continual political outrage. This is an advanced amnesia that can only lead to trouble. We can damage ourselves physically with the well-known ailments and diseases of ulcers and heart attacks. Numbing also has one more terrible impact. Distancing ourselves from our pain all too easily distances ourselves from others' pain. We get angry and judgmental instead of caring and compassionate.

Creative suffering through the losses means going directly into it, no matter what it is. We can be carrying true sadness or upset even though the loss was years ago. (The long-lasting impact of a loss is another similarity with compression.) We dwell with purpose and without complaining on the inner turmoil we feel about losing that cherished part of our life. Of course, we can share this sadness with friends and loved ones who care, to a point. Ultimately, however, it is only ours to bear. In this process, we stay with the sadness as long as is required, and until we need to access our more neutral and happy parts and get back to work, or to the kids, or to helping a friend put up the storm windows.

What can we learn about ourselves and life by this purposeful dwelling? Doesn't this just reinforce bad energy? Doesn't this just get us stuck? Isn't this the wallow problem?

The answer to all of the above is no, if we do our suffering well. The grief counselors know this, and the great religions teach this. Author and religious leader Karen Armstrong says, "All the world faiths put suffering at the top of their agenda, because it is an inescapable part of life."[1]

## EXAMPLE OF ONE WHO GETS IT

I have the honor to teach coaching skills at two dynamite coaching schools: at Columbia University and at my original coaching home, the Hudson Institute of Santa Barbara. At Columbia, I met a woman with ample human and coaching know-how by the name of Nicole Woodard, a former Wall Streeter with a heart of gold (yes, I know several of them).

Shortly after her graduation from the program, Nicole expressed her and her husband's joy over expecting a baby. When their son, Donovan, was born, Nicole's network of family and friends rejoiced with her.

Tragedy struck quickly. Little perfectly formed Donovan died at one day old, for reasons still not understood. Who can imagine the wrenching trauma of such a loss? I asked Nicole, whom I had stayed in touch with, if she would talk to me about her suffering and what it was teaching her. Here are a few things she graciously passed on:

66 I had to somehow move forward and keep Donovan's memory alive in a positive way. I had to not lose a part of myself, or define myself by this loss—is that what Donovan would have wanted, had he lived? I had to figure something out.

It is surprising who shows up for you in loss. Some whom I thought would, could not, or did not, because they did not know what to say. They did not know that it is just about being there—there is often no good thing to say.

As some time passed, I found that I moved from my deepest despair about me to seeing how life is very hard for so many others. I gained perspective that I had never had. My dad says that if you live long enough, you will lose somebody very dear to you. . . . Finally, more recently [seven months later], I started to get some desire back to reengage in normal, mundane stuff that had become meaningless for a long while.

I am getting some big lessons from all this. I am making meaning out of it and will for a long while. I am in some kind of new normal. It has been such a profound experience, and as I accept this, I am able to say I don't want to go back to the old normal, which couldn't happen anyway. I see that how I show up in loss and grief is how I show up generally, and I am not as hard on myself as I used to be. I am kinder and easier. Loss pushes you to change by giving you a different lens to look through.[2] 🙶

Nicole suffered, and will continue to suffer, creatively. By confronting the loss and staying in dialogue with her husband and herself, she took on the heavy pain of a broken heart. They planted a memorial tree on the Hudson for Donovan as one of many acts to help turn the ordeal into a meaningful segment of the new normal life they would never have chosen. This is the task for all of us—if not now, then sometime, and maybe often. As in the process for recalling and recasting a compression, Nicole works at interpreting her experience of the loss into hard-won wisdom without diminishing its mystery. She has arrived at a depth of compassion she would never have achieved otherwise.

Compassion, from the Latin meaning "to suffer with," may be the greatest gain of suffering well. Gibran said, "Your pain is the breaking of the shell that encloses your understanding."[3] If we go into the losses, we give our heart a chance to expand, to know real empathy for people of every kind. We are free to avoid this kind of gain, of course. If we choose to stay numb to the losses, we are quite capable of shrinking our heart.

## THREE PHASES OF CREATIVE SUFFERING

There are a few dos and don'ts to staying with the suffering.[4] Here is a big don't.

When absorbing the sadness of the loss, we must not concentrate on bad guys to demonize, or black holes of sympathy in which we get to play the cosmic victim of terrible circumstances. Demonizing and victimizing are the sources of those stories in which we can get so woefully stuck.

We need our heart in suffering for its capacities of courage and compassion, and our mind for extracting the meaning from the images of loss, the way we did in reclaiming and recasting. We let our heart go "heavy" for a time, not in a hopeless indefinite downspin, but in a way that we do feel real constriction in our chest. For those who have no clue or don't quite know (even though it sounds possible) what I am talking about, find a good body discipline person—a coach who understands the somatics of change is one example[5]—and work with him or her. And yes, guys, this means us; our gender is behind some on feeling what is going on with our hearts—with big exceptions, of course. If you experience bigger mood swings than most, be careful with this practice and monitor yourself for its impact. You should reread the warning on trauma in chapter 5.[6]

The constriction, the heaviness, is our heart energy at work, deepening into compassion. Physiologically speaking, this standing still with the sadness is some powerful neurotransmitter cocktail soaking our cells. It washes over us so that our brain won't get disconnected from our heart and do impressive heady things that make no heart sense, which we seem to like to do as a species. Candidates for lots-of-head/no-heart actions might include creating nuclear arsenals, designing complex financial instruments that no one understands, and creating substances that taste irresistibly good but have no nutritional value. You can make your own list; unfortunately, it can grow quite long.

Suffering well takes us through phases:

First, the suffering seems random, meaningless, maybe cruel or useless. We suffer as much from the suffering as from the original loss. The images of the old work patterns that so fit us or the person we loved overwhelm us. We have not started to absorb the suffering yet. *"Oh, I miss my old job . . . how I loved the travel, the camaraderie."*

Here it is important to do the following:

▶ Notice the images of loss and the feelings, without blame, and be patient.

▶ Disengage from any inner victim talk while maintaining empathy for yourself.

Second, after some time, and some of us are slow learners, we choose to absorb the loss. We can move on to an inevitable, if grudging, acceptance of our fate. We may even begin to feel ourselves stronger as a result of the suffering. We have started to absorb, not resist. We start to endure it with more grace, and certainly less suffering about the suffering. Our inner conversation shifts from one of grief to one of measured acceptance: *"Oh, I miss my old job and many of the roles that came with it; still, I feel so connected to my profession in good ways because of it."*

Here it is important to do the following:

▶ Forgive the bad actors if needed (and when you are ready).

▶ Be sensitive to new feelings and the reemergence of energies and tentative insights.

Third, we come to accept the suffering as an important part of our lives, as a process that deepens us and pulls us away from the shallower commitments of our doing and into the deeper levels of our being. We not only absorb the pain, but we transmute it into meaning and wisdom. *"Well, that job made me who I am today, and I am ready for what is next. I can go out now and do my own thing in the world, bringing the best of the old work with me."*

Here it is important to do the following:

▶ Use the images to elevate your story and provide meaning, claiming the wisdom acquired.

▶ Retell the story of your loss to serve others, or affirm your truth, with new possibilities.

**Eventually, we go beyond coping and enduring the suffering: we make meaning out of it and use it as a spiritual resource. The suffering that started off challenging our being and our ideas of what life is and should be ends up opening our heart, expanding our identity, and connecting us forever to the human family and life.**

Some of us got early training in the spiritual practice of suffering. From time to time, my nun teachers in grade school encouraged us to "give something up," the practice of forgoing an automatic creature comfort, a latte in a post-Starbucks world, a TV show, our favorite candy, any habit we had acquired. Giving up the good feeling of that habit created an irritant, a minor deprivation, and in the moments of feeling that deprivation, we absorbed a micro-suffering. During the irritation, we could pray—this was the "up" part of giving something up—so that our suffering could alleviate the suffering of others. We could have a higher thought or give the money that would have gone for the latte to the poor. Suffering consciously was about elevating our energy and tapping the better angels of our human nature.[7] With creative suffering, the nuns had us raise our thoughts from automatic and do something more loving and Christian, even if it was minor.

Much of this training in suffering was lost on us as kids, or it stayed dimly understood, if at all, as adults. For me, you can guess that through recall later in life, some with my old school friends, my adult spiritual imagination recast for me what the nuns were after. As I was getting lots of unwanted practice absorbing the losses coming at me in my life, I was able to move through the phases more deliberately. My own life got deeper, better, richer, when I became more acutely aware of my suffering—like that which came with excessive workloads stemming from my "straight A" compression, and certainly the biggest suffering of all, my loneliness as a father living apart from my sons.

All of the compressions and losses, big and small, have their own flavor, and so we learn and grow through them in different ways. All losses can teach compassion. Some teach autonomy. Others teach patience, persistence, generosity, interdependence, or courage. The type of loss carries the lesson. Creative and courageous suffering extracts the wisdom.

We can all eventually learn that suffering is its own gift. We need creative suffering now, as a conscious practice, for deepening our humanity when our consumer culture dulls our compassion with excess and hides us from our own depth.

## Collective Suffering as an Act of Expanding Love

On April 4, 1968, the day that Martin Luther King Jr. was assassinated, when the riots broke out in the urban cores across America, one city, Indianapolis, remained calm. It had the great fortune of hosting one man on a campaign trail, one who had learned how to suffer through the loss of an earlier assassination. Bobby Kennedy was scheduled to speak to a crowd in Indianapolis that day, and in this pre-Internet era, the large mixed-race crowd had not heard about Dr. King's death. The crowd was stunned by the tragic news as he started his comments.

Bobby had been advised not to speak, of course—what could he say on such a tragic occasion that could make any sense, and might it not even be dangerous? He decided to go ahead because he knew, two months before his own violent death, that he did have something to say about violence and death and the spirit of America. He gave a short speech that I have seen listed as one of the top 20 speeches in American history.

Bobby spoke of the impact of violence, the natural impulse to retribution, and he called on those present to suffer through the loss with love and forbearance. He shared his own earlier struggle. He cited the words of the Greek poet Aeschylus. The Greek poets had helped him find meaning in his suffering and reset himself after the loss of his brother John:

> Even in our sleep, pain, which cannot forget,
> Falls drop by drop upon the heart,
> Until in our despair and against our will,
> Comes wisdom through the awful grace of God.

In essence, what Bobby did that day was to transmute the anger and suffering of others through his already expanded heart. The crowd stayed calm as he appealed to their better angels even in the face of senseless violence.

In South Africa's effort to heal itself from the abominations of apartheid and to stop the cycle of retribution, it honored others' suffering at the Truth and Reconciliation Commission hearings. The country's wise leaders knew that suffering well takes us to a higher plane of our humanity, something not often enough seen in the loops of violence from which we seem unable to escape.While these may be big, dramatic examples, the principles are applicable to our own lives. We can lean into the suffering and allow our heart to make it something of value.

## LIVING ALONGSIDE THE MYSTERY OF SUFFERING

If this idea to confront loss seems too foreign to you, then don't do anything with the idea just yet. I did not come to this idea for a long time, and I had had some pretty good Christian training in suffering. You may not be able to accept it yet, but perhaps you can hold out for the possibility of someday seeing great value in your losses.

Just let the idea of using loss this way sit with you for a time and see what happens. We all have our own preferences here, and staying with suffering long enough to feel your heart expand and to sense the empathy and communion it engenders is the point. If you worked with evocations through reclaiming and compressions through recasting thus far, your imagination will be primed for the possibility.

Suffering is a mysterious affair—why are some of us asked, or required, to do more suffering than others? How much meaning can truly come from tragedy? Are some losses so great that destruction indeed outweighs any meaning? Even while addressing such unanswerable questions, let's not get over-the-top weepy and heavy. Suffering is too important to take overly seriously. The questions at the end of the chapter can help us to work our suffering-courageously muscles. When we are done absorbing and transmuting the pain, laughter becomes our elixir and we can do something light, maybe even silly.

After you have contemplated an image that weighed heavy on your heart, you might want to go to a superhero movie, visit a joke site on the Internet, or post a stupid picture on your profile. Be like the Irish at wakes who suffer loss and have a really good time. As the old description goes: "At your funeral, after they honor you with tears and kind words, they throw dirt on your face and go back to the house to eat potato salad."

Go deep with suffering, for the periods of time that you can handle and that are equal to what the impact of the compression deserves, and don't overdose.

## ▶SUMMARY

Loss leads to suffering. To some extent, the great religions and psychology have addressed the purpose, process, and impacts of suffering, But it is up to each of us to make our own peace with the questions and dilemmas that only suffering can bring into our lives. Losing beloved parts of our lives and ourselves is never easy, but it can carry meaning if we have courage and patience. When our mind and heart extract meaning out of suffering, sometimes in spite of ourselves, we can endure dark times. We can foster a capacity for resilience that is a resource for a lifetime.

▷ **Core takeaway idea:** Remembrance prepares us for many things, including the second half of life, when we grow by confronting our losses soulfully.

## ▶ STATEMENTS OF INTENT TO ENGAGE THE WILL AND FIRE THE IMAGINATION

Transforming losses into permanent life lessons, for myself and others, is a gift to the world that only I, with my particular story, can make happen.

I combine the brutal truth of not sugarcoating what I have endured with my happy heritage of evocations in order to extract soulful elements from every life and career chapter.

The hurts I have absorbed are gifts, providing me opportunities to learn lasting resilience and accumulate wisdom.

## ▶ EXERCISE

Answer the questions that make you think about your losses the most creatively and the most courageously.

- ▶ What cherished part of your life have you lost recently or will you lose before too long?
- ▶ What phase of the suffering are you in?
  - Coping, or resisting and hoping it will go away.
  - Absorbing its impact even if it makes little sense yet.
  - Accepting it and feeling somehow stronger and able to move on.

- ▶ What lessons have losses taught you to this point?
- ▶ What is your favorite scar, your most fruitful failure?

# Notes

## Introduction: Your Past Can Work for You

1. Bill George with Peter Sims, *True North: Discover Your Authentic Leadership* (New York: John Wiley & Sons, 2007), 71, 72.
2. Eckhart Tolle, *The Power of Now* (Novato, CA: New World Library, 1999), ix.
3. George Santayana, *The Life of Reason, or The Phases of Human Progress*, Vol. *1 of 4*, Classic Reprint (Charleston, SC: Forgotten Books, www.forgottenbooks.org, 2010), 284.
4. There are forms of therapy called ahistorical because they do not use, and even avoid going into, our past. Some of us really like to stick with our fixed stories. Doug Silsbee's *Presence-Based Coaching: Cultivating Self-Generative Leaders Through Mind, Body, and Heart* (San Francisco: Jossey-Bass, 2009) is the best book I know for describing how our past can leave us habituated and stuck.
5. See Tommy Emmanuel C.G.P (www.tommyemmanuel.com).
6. Tommy Emmanuel, interview by the author, March 2010.
7. Fur Peace Ranch (www.furpeaceranch.com).

## Chapter 1, The Underused Past: The Price of Forgotten Yesterdays

1. Tolle, *The Power of Now*.
2. Carl Sandburg, *The Complete Poems of Carl Sandburg*, rev. and exp. ed. (New York: Harcourt, 2003).

3. One favorite tactic of the people who make their money stirring up controversy with very strong views is to create a shallow version of a position they disagree with so that they can make fun of it. That is not my attempt here. There is much to be said for staying fully in the moment, philosophically and psychologically. I cited Doug Silsbee's book *Presence-Based Coaching* earlier, and there are others. But I will take issue with the extremes.

4. Manfred F. R. Kets de Vries, *Coach and Couch: The Psychology of Making Better Leaders* (New York: Macmillan/INSEAD Business Press, 2010), 4.

5. Thomas Moore's books, such as *Care of the Soul: A Guide for Cultivating Depth and Sacredness in Everyday Life* (New York: HarperCollins, 1992), are full of thoughts on how reflection and memory can help us, as well as on common mistakes, such as pathologizing our past. Philip Zimbardo's *The Time Paradox: The New Psychology of Time That Will Change Your Life* (New York: Free Press, 2008) is a helpful look at how we have time perspective "styles" that influence us.

6. The case of Bill here reminds me of the entire field of Appreciative Inquiry, which developed around change efforts at the individual, organization, and community levels. Diana Whitney and David Cooperrider write useful practical books in this field, such as *Appreciative Inquiry: A Positive Revolution in Change* (San Francisco: Berrett-Koehler, 1999).

7. In *Stumbling on Happiness* (New York: Alfred A. Knopf, 2006; 155), Harvard's Daniel Gilbert gives us a clue as to why we stay stuck in misuses of the past: "Rats and pigeons may respond to stimuli as they are *presented* in the world, people respond to stimuli as they are *represented* in the mind." We make up logical-sounding reasons for our misinterpretations.

8. Pat Conroy, *The Prince of Tides* (New York: Dial Press, 2002).

### Chapter 2, Good and Bad News: Evoked and Compressed

1. Stephen Gill, ed., *William Wordsworth: The Major Works* (New York: Oxford University Press, 2008), 299.

2. Eugene O'Neill, *Long Day's Journey into Night*, 2nd ed. (New Haven, CT: Yale University Press, 2002).

3. Author, teacher, and psychoanalyst James Hollis, in all of his books, was the number one influence in my realizing how I had sugarcoated my past. Read his books on midlife if you want to hear his argument. I owe much of this section to his catalytic impact in my life.

4. Much has been written about the Ignatian exercises. For more information on this 400-year-old Christian recall process, contact your closest Jesuit university (there are 27 in the United States, and many more internationally). Or visit this Wikipedia page, http://en.wikipedia.org/wiki/List_of_Jesuit_institutions, to find them. You need not go away for 30 days, as there are other ways to complete the process.

5. André Delbecq, interview with the author, June 2008.

## Chapter 3, Recall

1. Barbara Kingsolver, *Animal Dreams: A Novel* (New York: Harper-Perennial, 2003), 280.

2. Gifford Pinchot and Ron Pellman, *Intrapreneuring in Action: A Handbook for Business Innovation* (San Francisco: Berrett-Koehler, 1999).

3. Gifford Pinchot, interview with the author, July 2008.

4. Valerie Morris, interview with the author, May 2008.

5. Suppressing memories through disassociation with your experience is always a possibility. You may want to find a therapist, who will want to know your motives, to work with you on memory recall. One famous woman whose brain has been studied extensively can't not remember almost every detail in her life, a huge burden.

6. Conroy, *The Prince of Tides*.

7. David Ricoh, *When the Past Is Present: Healing the Emotional Wounds That Sabotage Our Relationships* (Boston: Shambhala Press, 2008), 4.

## Chapter 4, Reclaim

1. The one I like the most in dealing with our histories is *Leadership Passages: The Personal and Professional Transitions That Make or Break a Leader* (San Francisco: Jossey-Bass, 2004).

2. David Dotlich, interview by the author, May 2008.

3. Barbara Roberts, interview by the author, October 2009.

4. M. K. Larson, interview by the author, July 2008.
5. John P. Schuster, *Answering Your Call: A Guide to Living Your Deepest Purpose* (San Francisco: Berrett-Koehler, 2003).
6. Conroy, *The Prince of Tides*.
7. Thomas Moore, *The Soul's Religion: Cultivating a Profoundly Spiritual Way of Life* (San Francisco: HarperCollins, 2002), 19.

## Chapter 5, Recast

1. Paul Hoover, "Theory of Margins," from *Winter (Mirror)* (Chicago: Flood Editions, 2002).
2. Wikipedia's article "Defence mechanism" (http://en.wikipedia.org/wiki/Defence_mechanism) is a primer on how our defense mechanisms are at play. Healthy people all use them, and it only gets unhealthy when we overdo them.
3. John Pepper, *What Really Matters: Reflections on My Career at Procter & Gamble with Guiding Principles for Success in the Marketplace and in Life* (Cincinnati, OH: Procter & Gamble, 2005), 9.
4. Pepper, *What Really Matters*, 10.
5. Joe Cunningham, interview with the author, June 2007.
6. Jack Mezirow, "Perspective Transformation," *Adult Education Quarterly* 28, no. 2 (January 1978), 100. Mezirow wrote, "[Perspective change] . . . implies a conscious recognition of the difference between one's old viewpoint and the new one and a decision to appropriate the newer perspective as being of more value. Of course, there are wide variations in individual personality that influence one's ability to experience such growth. When serious internal inhibitions impair normal development, an adult may require therapy rather than education. Conceptualizing one's self concept in the process of perspective taking is developmentally a function of maturity."
7. Khaled Hosseini, *The Kite Runner* (New York: Riverhead Books, 2003), 1.
8. A resource for people who tend to brood negatively on their past: *The Mindful Path Through Worry and Rumination: Letting Go of Anxious and Depressive Thoughts*, by Sameet M. Kumar (Oakland, CA: New Harbinger, 2009).

## Chapter 6, Answering the Big Question: When to Say Yes and No

1. Don DeLillo, *The Names* (New York: Vintage, 1989).
2. Cheryl Kravitz, interview by the author, January 2009.
3. Jorma Kaukonen, interview by the author, April 2010.

## Chapter 7, Using Suffering to Grow

1. Karen Armstrong, *The Spiral Staircase: My Climb Out of Darkness* (New York: Anchor Books, 2004), 272.
2. Nicole Woodard, interview with the author, April 2010.
3. Kahlil Gibran, *The Prophet* (Sydney, Australia: Phone Media, 2002), 52.
4. Useful contemporary reading on suffering: from Pema Chödrön, a Buddhist, *When Things Fall Apart: Heart Advice for Difficult Times* (Boston: Shambhala, 2002), and Thomas Moore, a Christian, *The Soul's Religion: Cultivating a Profoundly Spiritual Way of Life* (New York: Perennial, 2003). And C. S. Lewis's *The Problem of Pain* (San Francisco: Harper SanFrancisco, 2001) is a classic.
5. Silsbee, *Presence-Based Coaching.*
6. I am much in favor of medicine for those with mood swings, having witnessed the excessive suffering of those fighting a shortage of the right neurotransmitters.
7. The Buddhist name for taking on the suffering of others is *tonglen.*

# Acknowledgments

I HAVE MANY to thank. I put Johanna Vondeling and Steve Piersanti of Berrett-Koehler first. What support and challenge they provided! I felt the whole team at BK behind me, including the reviewers—Amol Ray, for amnesia ideas; Jill Swensen, for lovingly chewing up my writing; Charlotte Ashlock, sparkling with enthusiastic counterthought; and Dan Schatz, for wisdom—and Elissa Rabellino, for making copyediting fun.

My friend Kelly Gerling always listens deeply to my ideas. My Hudson Institute team did much to encourage me. Special thanks to Pam McLean, our leader; Kathleen Stinnett, for reviewing early versions; and Pat Adson, super therapist, for all the collaboration. Barbara Roberts is a special example of the core message of the book. Anne Power came through in special ways as always, along with my Columbia U. colleagues. All my Merryck and Co. buddies have great stories, and Nick Hill, a client who models so much about excellence, is living his.

Thanks for the gift of time to all whom I interviewed—including André Delbecq, a mentor's mentor; Valerie Morris; John Pepper; M. K. Larson; David Dotlich; Gifford Pinchot; Tommy Emmanuel and Jorma Kaukonen, guitar gods who inspire; Cheryl Kravitz; and all those I surveyed, including cousin Joe Cunningham, Colleen Mizuki, and more.

My sisters, Elaine and Mary Ann, share so many memories with me—thanks for such great recalling to them and to my Schuster cousins, stretching from Dubuque to Portland. Thanks to my dear friends from old school haunts in Omaha, Cheyenne, and Cincinnati, who could not have given me a better storehouse of memories. Special thanks to Joe Vacanti and Dave Quammen.

Big thanks to my sons, Jeff and Dave, in whose stories I continue. Dave, thanks for the research on memory and more. Most of all, thanks to Patricia, super-partner wife and friend, a memory maker and weaver. Looks like more memories to generate, lady.

# Index

# About the Author

JOHN SCHUSTER IS an author and mentor/coach (www
.johnpschuster.com), and has co-owned a speaking and
training firm for 25-plus years (www.skalliance.com and
www.profitandcash.com). He is a faculty member for Coach
Certification Programs at Columbia University and the Hudson Institute of Santa Barbara, and he is pursuing a certificate
in Jungian studies from Saybrook University. He is also a
coach for Merryck & Company, a CEO-mentoring firm, and
works for nonprofit and government organizations.

John is the author of such books as *Answering Your
Call: A Guide to Living Your Deepest Purpose* (Berrett-
Koehler Publishers, 2003), *Hum-Drum to Hot-Diggity on
Leadership* (Steadfast Publishers, 2001), and two books on
open-book management. His clients include the American
Academy of Family Physicians, corporations and hospitals,
and many smaller and midsize organizations.

John is a green advocate; pursues gardening, tennis, and
guitar; and has three grandchildren. He is married to his
business partner, Patricia Kane. He believes in learning
communities, sustainability, and local food. He works to
create markets and communities that foster human possibilities, and he naps whenever possible.

Also by John P. Schuster

# Answering Your Call
## A Guide for Living Your Deepest Purpose

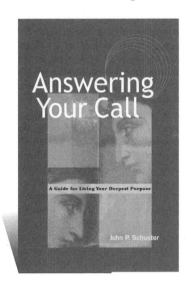

Do you feel like you were put on this earth to reach for something beyond the traditional definitions of success? Do you have a higher calling? John Schuster describes what it means to be "called"—to live a life that fully uses your talents and adds the most lasting value to the world. Drawing on real-world examples, he offers principles and guidelines for finding the courage to respond to your call, staying on track to make your vision a reality, and dealing with saboteurs who try to squelch your dreams of living a "called" life. *Answering Your Call* provides exercises that appeal to our practical side as well as inspirational examples from history and literature. It is a spiritual how-to book about discerning what it is that the world needs you to do.

Paperback, 168 pages, ISBN 978-1-57675-205-0
PDF ebook, ISBN 978-1-57675-959-2

Berrett–Koehler Publishers, Inc.
San Francisco, *www.bkconnection.com*          **800.929.2929**

# Berrett–Koehler
## Publishers

Berrett-Koehler is an independent publisher dedicated to an ambitious mission: *Creating a World That Works for All.*

We believe that to truly create a better world, action is needed at all levels—individual, organizational, and societal. At the individual level, our publications help people align their lives with their values and with their aspirations for a better world. At the organizational level, our publications promote progressive leadership and management practices, socially responsible approaches to business, and humane and effective organizations. At the societal level, our publications advance social and economic justice, shared prosperity, sustainability, and new solutions to national and global issues.

A major theme of our publications is "Opening Up New Space." Berrett-Koehler titles challenge conventional thinking, introduce new ideas, and foster positive change. Their common quest is changing the underlying beliefs, mindsets, institutions, and structures that keep generating the same cycles of problems, no matter who our leaders are or what improvement programs we adopt.

We strive to practice what we preach—to operate our publishing company in line with the ideas in our books. At the core of our approach is stewardship, which we define as a deep sense of responsibility to administer the company for the benefit of all of our "stakeholder" groups: authors, customers, employees, investors, service providers, and the communities and environment around us.

We are grateful to the thousands of readers, authors, and other friends of the company who consider themselves to be part of the "BK Community." We hope that you, too, will join us in our mission.

### A BK Life Book

This book is part of our BK Life series. BK Life books change people's lives. They help individuals improve their lives in ways that are beneficial for the families, organizations, communities, nations, and world in which they live and work. To find out more, visit **www.bk-life.com**.

# Berrett–Koehler
# Publishers

A community dedicated to creating
a world that works for all

## Visit Our Website: www.bkconnection.com

Read book excerpts, see author videos and Internet movies, read our authors' blogs, join discussion groups, download book apps, find out about the BK Affiliate Network, browse subject-area libraries of books, get special discounts, and more!

## Subscribe to Our Free E-Newsletter, the *BK Communiqué*

Be the first to hear about new publications, special discount offers, exclusive articles, news about bestsellers, and more! Get on the list for our free e-newsletter by going to **www.bkconnection.com**.

## Get Quantity Discounts

Berrett-Koehler books are available at quantity discounts for orders of ten or more copies. Please call us toll-free at (800) 929-2929 or email us at bkp.orders@aidcvt.com.

## Join the BK Community

BKcommunity.com is a virtual meeting place where people from around the world can engage with kindred spirits to create a world that works for all. BKcommunity.com members may create their own profiles, blog, start and participate in forums and discussion groups, post photos and videos, answer surveys, announce and register for upcoming events, and chat with others online in real time. Please join the conversation!